I0014537

Web3, Blockchain, And NFTs for Beginners

A Non-Technical Guide to
Decentralized Identity, Token
Communities, and Digital Ownership

Nathan Terrence

Contents

Chapter 1: Getting Started

Introduction

From the moment we learned to send an email, stream a movie, or buy a concert ticket online, the internet has been woven into our everyday lives. We shop, socialize, learn, and entertain ourselves on platforms that have become second nature—so much so that it's hard to imagine a time before social media or streaming services. But behind the scenes, the internet is entering its next phase: **Web3**.

You may have heard the buzzwords—blockchain, NFTs, crypto—but what do they really mean for ordinary people? Contrary to popular belief, Web3 isn't solely about speculative investments or obscure digital collectibles. Rather, it represents a fundamental shift in how data, identity, and value move across the internet. Instead of big tech companies owning and controlling our online experiences, **Web3 enables us—the users—to own our data and participate in communities on our own terms**.

Yet, for many who lack a technical background, Web3 can feel like navigating a maze of jargon. Explaining concepts like "decentralized identity" or "smart contracts" in simple terms is often overlooked in favor of more advanced developer conversations. That's why this book exists: **to demystify Web3 for everyone**.

Why Now?

We're at a point in internet history where conversations about privacy, data ownership, and digital rights are more crucial than ever. Many feel uneasy about how much power major tech platforms hold over our personal information, online identities, and social interactions. Web3 offers a possible solution by distributing control and rewarding participation in ways that traditional, centralized platforms can't match.

Who Is This Book For?

If you're curious about the next evolution of the internet but feel overwhelmed by technical details or flashy crypto headlines, this book is for you. We'll break down the **core ideas of Web3— decentralized identity, token-based communities, and user-owned data—into plain language**, using real-world examples and approachable explanations. Whether you're a casual internet user, a small business owner, a creative professional, or simply someone who wants to make more informed online choices, this guide will walk you through the fundamentals of Web3 without unnecessary complexity.

What You'll Learn

- **The Evolution of the Web**: From static pages (Web1) to centralized platforms (Web2) and finally toward user-driven, decentralized networks (Web3).

- **Blockchain & Smart Contracts**: Why these technologies matter, how they work at a high level, and what they enable in everyday life.

- **Decentralized Identity**: How to take control of your online persona and protect your data in a self-sovereign way.

- **Token-Based Communities & DAOs**: How communities form around shared goals using digital tokens for membership and governance, and how you can join or even start one.

- **Privacy & Data Ownership**: Practical tools and tips for handling your information securely, so you remain in the driver's seat.

- **Real-World Applications**: Discover how Web3 can help you unlock new opportunities—creative, financial, and personal—by letting you own and control your assets and interactions online.

How to Use This Book

Think of **Demystifying Web3** as a friendly tour guide through unknown territory. We'll begin by exploring the background of the internet's evolution, then dive into the specific building blocks of Web3. We'll connect these topics to real-life scenarios and walk you through setting up the tools you need to explore this new digital landscape. Each section builds on the last, so feel free to read it cover to cover or skip around to the topics that interest you most.

By the end of this book, you won't just know what Web3 is—you'll understand why it matters, how it works in practice, and what steps you can take to seize its benefits. The promise of a more open, user-centric internet isn't just for developers or tech enthusiasts. It's for all of us, and it starts here. Let's begin our journey toward a web where we truly **own** our data, identities, and online experiences.

Chapter 2: The Evolution of the Web

2.1 Web1: The Read-Only Era

The story of the World Wide Web begins modestly, with static pages of information and a small community of researchers and hobbyists. Though it's often referred to as **Web1**, that term was not invented until well after its heyday. At the time, no one said "I'm browsing Web1!" because no one had the perspective that the web would continue to evolve in waves. Still, looking back at the early internet of the 1990s, we see a foundational moment in modern history—one that gave birth to a revolutionary means of connecting people, sharing knowledge, and enabling entirely new forms of communication.

Early Foundations and the Role of ARPANET

To understand Web1, we need to reach back even

further, to the late 1960s and 1970s, when the U.S. Department of Defense funded the creation of **ARPANET** (Advanced Research Projects Agency Network). ARPANET was not the web, but rather one of the earliest packet-switching networks—a means of sending chunks of data, called packets, between computers. Universities, research institutions, and government agencies used ARPANET primarily for academic and defense research. It was the backbone upon which much of internet technology was refined.

Fast-forward a couple of decades, and by the late 1980s, the internet was still primarily a tool for researchers, scientists, and technically inclined individuals who communicated using text-based protocols like **FTP (File Transfer Protocol)**, **Telnet**, and **Gopher**. There was no unified system for navigating from one set of online documents to another, no consistent way to link from a piece of text in one file to a piece of text in another file somewhere else in the world—until a man named

Tim Berners-Lee introduced the concept of the **World Wide Web** at CERN (the European Organization for Nuclear Research) in 1989.

Tim Berners-Lee and the Birth of the Web

Berners-Lee proposed an innovative idea: a system for hyperlinked documents, accessible over the internet. This approach allowed users to click on text-based "links" to jump from one document to another, even if those documents resided on different servers in different geographic locations. By 1990, Berners-Lee had developed the essential building blocks:

- **HTML (HyperText Markup Language)**: A markup language for creating structured documents with hyperlinks.

- **HTTP (Hypertext Transfer Protocol)**: A protocol for transferring HTML documents across the internet.

- **URI/URL (Uniform Resource Identifier/Locator)**: An addressing system so that any resource on the web could be uniquely identified and retrieved.

It's hard to overstate how revolutionary this was. Suddenly, it became possible to create and navigate a global network of interlinked digital "pages," each containing text and, eventually, images. Berners-Lee's inventions led to the creation of the first web browser, called **WorldWideWeb** (later renamed Nexus), which he developed on a NeXT computer. However, it was the release of the **Mosaic** browser in 1993—created by Marc Andreessen and his team at the National Center for Supercomputing Applications (NCSA)—that helped popularize the web for a wider audience.

Characteristics of Web1

When we talk about Web1 as the "read-only" era, we're primarily referring to the fact that average users **consumed** information rather than contributed it. There was limited interactivity. You might visit a web page, read the text, perhaps see some images, and then move on to another page. Here are some of the hallmark features of that time:

1. **Static HTML Pages**: Most websites were built with raw HTML files. The content would not change unless the webmaster manually updated the HTML.

2. **Limited Multimedia**: Early sites were typically text-heavy. Images were often compressed or very small, and embedding video or audio was extremely uncommon due to slow connection speeds.

3. **Narrow Participation**: While the web was technically open for anyone to join, creating a website in those days required some technical skill. You had to learn HTML, figure out how to host files on a server, and often rely on dial-up internet connections.

4. **Lack of Interactivity**: Forums and

bulletin board systems (BBSs) did exist, but for the most part, interactions were limited. Websites did not typically encourage users to comment on articles, submit content, or "like" anything.

Despite these constraints, Web1 did something extraordinary: it **democratized access to information**. For the first time, an individual in one part of the world could publish content that someone else halfway across the globe could read within seconds—at minimal cost. This was a major leap from the days of specialized database terminals or libraries, and it opened up new possibilities for research, education, and, eventually, commerce.

Commercialization and the Dot-Com Boom

As more people discovered the web, entrepreneurs and companies began to recognize its enormous potential. By the mid-1990s, the first e-commerce sites emerged. Booksellers like **Amazon** (founded in 1994) and auction platforms like **eBay** (founded in 1995) offered a glimpse into how the internet could transform business. These early forays into online retail began to shift the web from a purely informational resource into a platform where buying and selling became possible.

The **dot-com boom** of the late 1990s brought in massive investments. Countless startups sprang up, offering everything from web portals (like Yahoo!) to specialized search engines, online magazines, and more. By 1999, the hype had reached such a peak that almost any company with a ".com" in its name could attract significant venture capital, even if its business model was shaky or nonexistent.

Although this period ended dramatically with the **dot-com crash** of 2000–2001—when many internet startups went bankrupt—it nevertheless accelerated the adoption of the web worldwide. Millions more people gained their first exposure to the internet, and the idea of using websites for both information and commerce became cemented in popular culture.

Limitations and the Seeds of Change

Despite its success in spreading information, Web1 remained mostly a "read-only" affair. If you were an ordinary user, creating content online might involve building a personal GeoCities page, writing HTML in a text editor, and then uploading it via FTP. This was not particularly user-friendly, and it meant that the vast majority of web users remained consumers of content rather than contributors.

Moreover, internet speeds were quite slow—dial-up modems typically ranged from 14.4 kbps to 56 kbps. Downloading even a single high-resolution image could take minutes. Video streaming, a routine part of daily life now, was practically impossible without specialized plugins and a lot of patience.

Yet, the seeds of a more interactive web were already being planted. Technologies like **JavaScript** (introduced in the mid-1990s) allowed small interactive elements on web pages. A handful of pioneering sites offered forums or "guestbooks," letting visitors post short messages. This foreshadowed the massive changes to come.

The Legacy of Web1

Web1 gave the world a fundamental shift: an open, global platform for information exchange. Even if it was often slow, limited, and text-centric, it sparked imaginations and opened the door to an age of constant connectivity. The lessons learned during Web1's reign—about open standards, the power of hyperlinks, and the global appetite for information—would serve as a launching pad for the next stage of internet evolution: **Web2**.

Web1's read-only nature also underscored the limitations of a purely one-way internet. People wanted to do more than just read; they wanted to interact, share, collaborate, and participate. The idea that the internet could be more than a digital library—maybe a global conversation—set the stage for the interactive explosion that would define the next decade.

2.2 Web2: The Interactive & Centralized Era

By the early 2000s, the foundations laid by Web1 were poised for transformation. The notion that users should be able to contribute as well as consume had become increasingly evident. Faster internet speeds (broadband), more powerful computers, and the proliferation of easy-to-use software tools all converged to create a new paradigm: **Web2**. While there isn't a precise start date for Web2, its ethos of interactivity, user-generated content, and social connectivity distinguishes it from the read-only architecture of Web1.

Key Innovations Driving Web2

1. **Broadband and Improved Speeds**: As cable modems, DSL, and eventually fiber-optic connections became more widespread,

people no longer had to endure excruciatingly slow downloads. This facilitated richer media experiences— images, music, and, crucially, video.

2. **Rise of Social Media Platforms**: Sites like **MySpace** (launched in 2003) and **Facebook** (launched in 2004) fundamentally changed how people used the internet. Instead of just reading content, users actively posted statuses, photos, videos, and formed online communities.

3. **User-Generated Content**: Platforms like **YouTube** (founded in 2005) allowed everyday people to share videos with a global audience, transforming the media landscape. Blogging platforms such as **Blogger** and **WordPress** made it simple for non-technical users to publish their own articles and essays.

4. **Ajax and Rich Web Applications**: The

mid-2000s saw the popularization of **Ajax** (Asynchronous JavaScript and XML), enabling webpages to update data dynamically without needing a full refresh. This paved the way for more fluid web apps, such as Google Maps and Gmail, which felt faster and more responsive than traditional Web1 pages.

Chapter 3: Key Building Blocks of Web3

The term **Web3** is often associated with buzzwords like blockchain, crypto, decentralization, and NFTs. But behind the hype lies a genuine technological and cultural shift in how the internet operates. To understand this shift, we need to dive into the **building blocks** that make Web3 possible. Unlike earlier versions of the web, which depended on centralized servers and a handful of dominant platform providers, Web3 aspires to create a more **democratic, user-owned, and resilient** digital environment. To achieve this, Web3 relies on four essential technological components:

1. **Blockchain Basics**: A method of recording data on a distributed ledger in a way that is transparent, secure, and tamper-resistant.

2. **Tokens and Cryptocurrencies**: Digital assets that incentivize network participation

and represent value, membership, or unique properties.

3. **Smart Contracts**: Self-executing agreements that live on the blockchain and automate processes without intermediaries.

4. **Decentralized Apps (dApps) and Protocols**: Software applications and underlying protocols that leverage blockchain, tokens, and smart contracts to deliver services without relying on centralized authorities.

In this chapter, we'll explore each building block in depth, providing both technical explanations and real-world examples. By the end, you should have a comprehensive grasp of **how** these components fit together to form a new kind of internet—and **why** it matters for users, developers, and society at large.

3.1 Blockchain Basics

A Brief History of Ledgers and Trust

Humans have relied on ledgers for centuries to keep track of transactions—whether those transactions involve money, goods, or property titles. Traditionally, a trusted third party, such as a bank or government office, maintained and verified these ledgers. This centralized model worked as long as we trusted the gatekeepers to do their jobs honestly.

With the rise of digital technology, however, it became clear that **digital information is easy to copy, alter, or delete**. If you store a financial database in a single location, hackers, corrupt insiders, or software bugs can potentially compromise that data. This vulnerability led innovators to seek a more robust and trust-minimized system.

Enter the Blockchain

A **blockchain** is often described as a "distributed ledger" or a "chain of blocks." Each block in the chain groups together a set of verified transactions or data entries. Once a block is finalized, it is appended to the previous block, creating a chronological, tamper-evident record. The decentralized nature of blockchain means that **thousands or even millions of computers**— called **nodes**—keep copies of this ledger. No single node controls the database. Instead, they reach consensus on what the correct version of the ledger is through specialized algorithms.

This approach solves a fundamental problem in computer science known as the **double-spend** or "Byzantine Generals" problem, which asks: How can independent actors in a network agree on a single version of truth without trusting any single authority? Satoshi Nakamoto's 2008 white paper on **Bitcoin** famously introduced the blockchain as a practical solution to this conundrum.

Key Characteristics

1. **Decentralization**: Instead of one central server, many nodes around the world

maintain the database, making it extremely resilient.

2. **Immutability**: Once data is recorded on the chain, altering it becomes computationally expensive or impossible, providing a historical record that is hard to tamper with.

3. **Transparency**: Public blockchains allow anyone to view the entire ledger's history, which can be verified independently by users and third parties.

4. **Security**: Through cryptographic techniques like hashing and digital signatures, blockchain ensures that only valid transactions make it onto the ledger.

Consensus Mechanisms

One of the most vital aspects of any blockchain is its **consensus mechanism**—the method by which nodes agree that a block of transactions is valid.

Two prominent mechanisms include:

- **Proof of Work (PoW)**: Used by Bitcoin, PoW requires "miners" to solve computationally difficult puzzles. This process is energy-intensive and forms a key security layer, but it can be criticized for its environmental impact.

- **Proof of Stake (PoS)**: Employed by newer blockchains such as Ethereum (following its 2022 merge event), Cardano, and others, PoS requires validators to "stake" (lock up) tokens as collateral to propose and validate new blocks. This approach is typically more energy-efficient.

There are other consensus models, such as **Delegated Proof of Stake (DPoS)**, **Proof of Authority (PoA)**, and **Byzantine Fault Tolerance (BFT)** variants, each with trade-offs in terms of security, scalability, and decentralization.

On-Chain vs. Off-Chain Data

Not everything needs to be stored directly on the blockchain. Some data—like large files, photos, or videos—can be impractical to store on-chain due to space and cost constraints. In such cases, **off-chain** solutions like the **InterPlanetary File System (IPFS)** or other decentralized storage systems are used, while the blockchain only stores references or "hashes" to these files. This architecture keeps the blockchain's size manageable while still benefiting from the security and immutability of a decentralized ledger.

Real-World Examples

1. **Bitcoin**: The first and most well-known blockchain, primarily used for peer-to-peer digital cash.

2. **Ethereum**: Introduced the concept of smart contracts, enabling a broader range of decentralized applications.

3. **Public vs. Private Blockchains**: Enterprises sometimes use permissioned or

private blockchains (Hyperledger Fabric, R3 Corda) for supply chain tracking, financial settlements, and business logistics, where only known participants can validate transactions.

Why Blockchain Matters for Web3

In the context of Web3, blockchains serve as the **trustless, decentralized backbone** on which new applications are built. Rather than relying on a central authority to manage a user database or digital assets, these responsibilities are distributed among network participants. This offers:

- Greater user autonomy and ownership.

- Reduced dependence on tech giants for authentication and data security.

- A transparent record of transactions and interactions, which can foster trust in online communities and marketplaces.

Blockchain technology thus underpins the ethos of

Web3: building an internet where **ownership, governance, and value** can be shared among all participants.

3.2 Tokens and Cryptocurrencies

If blockchains are the databases of Web3, then **tokens** are the data entries that store and represent various forms of value or utility. **Cryptocurrencies**, the most recognized type of blockchain token, first gained mainstream attention with Bitcoin's meteoric rise. However, the world of tokens extends far beyond digital cash. In Web3, tokens can represent anything from ownership shares and governance rights to exclusive membership perks or digital collectibles.

What Are Tokens?

A token is, in essence, a digital unit recorded on a blockchain. It can be **fungible** (interchangeable with other units) or **non-fungible** (unique and indivisible). Fungible tokens work like traditional currencies: one dollar is the same as any other dollar. Non-fungible tokens (NFTs), on the other hand, are unique assets—no two are precisely alike, just like distinct works of art.

Cryptocurrencies vs. Other Types of Tokens

The term **cryptocurrency** generally refers to a fungible token that serves as a medium of exchange, store of value, or unit of account, similar to traditional money. But Web3's token landscape is more diverse:

- **Utility Tokens**: Grant holders access to a specific service or product. They might be used to pay for transaction fees on a blockchain network or to access premium features in a decentralized app.

- **Security Tokens**: Represent real-world financial assets, such as stocks, bonds, or real estate shares. These tokens are subject to securities regulations.

- **Governance Tokens**: Allow holders to vote on proposals within a decentralized organization or protocol. They are crucial in **DAOs (Decentralized Autonomous Organizations)**.

- **Non-Fungible Tokens (NFTs)**: Represent unique items such as digital art, collectibles, or in-game assets. Their core trait is uniqueness and indivisibility.

The Role of Scarcity and Incentives

One key reason tokens have gained prominence is because they **create digital scarcity**. On a blockchain like Ethereum, token creation and transfers follow strict rules enforced by smart contracts. This means no central entity can arbitrarily inflate the token supply or reverse transactions.

Such predictability and scarcity provide **strong incentives** for community participation. For instance, in a decentralized file storage network, tokens might be awarded to users who provide unused hard drive space. Similarly, in a play-to-earn game, users can gain tokens by spending time playing or completing challenges, and these tokens might have real-world value on crypto exchanges.

How Tokens Are Created

On many blockchains, creating a new token can be as simple as writing a smart contract. For instance, Ethereum uses the **ERC-20 standard** for fungible tokens. This standard outlines a set of rules and functions—like how balances are tracked, how tokens are transferred, and how to get the total supply. For NFTs, **ERC-721** (or the newer **ERC-1155**) is the standard. By following these templates, developers can create custom tokens that are immediately compatible with wallets and exchanges across the ecosystem.

Token Distribution Methods

- **Initial Coin Offerings (ICOs)**: Popular in 2017, ICOs allowed projects to raise funds by selling newly created tokens. Many regulators viewed ICOs similarly to unregistered securities offerings, leading to increased scrutiny.

- **Airdrops**: Tokens are distributed (often for free) to holders of another token or to members of a community, usually for marketing or community-building purposes.

- **Mining and Staking**: In proof-of-work systems, miners earn newly minted coins by validating blocks. In proof-of-stake systems, validators earn staking rewards in proportion to their staked tokens.

- **Play-to-Earn and Engagement**: Tokens can be rewarded to users for playing blockchain-based games or contributing to online communities, reflecting a shift toward user-centric monetization models.

Real-World Use Cases

1. **Payment and Remittances**: Cryptocurrencies like Bitcoin and stablecoins like USDC or DAI facilitate cross-border payments at lower fees than traditional banking.

2. **Digital Art and Collectibles**: NFTs revolutionized how artists can sell unique digital works. Platforms like OpenSea, Rarible, and Foundation have become major marketplaces for such assets.

3. **Community Governance**: Projects like MakerDAO use governance tokens (MKR) to let community members vote on protocol changes, interest rates, and other key decisions.

4. **Gaming**: Axie Infinity, The Sandbox, and other blockchain-based games offer native tokens for trading in-game assets or participating in governance.

Opportunities and Risks

- **Opportunities**: Tokens can democratize access to investing, enable grassroots fundraising, and create new business models for digital creators. They also align incentives between project teams and communities, fostering loyalty and collaboration.

- **Risks**: Volatility remains a significant issue; token prices can swing wildly. Regulatory uncertainty also looms large, with governments still figuring out how to classify and tax different token types. Scams and rug pulls (where token creators abandon a project after raising funds) can harm investors and tarnish the industry's image.

Why Tokens Matter for Web3

Tokens are essential to **Web3's promise** of an internet owned by its users. They turn abstract network usage or community participation into something tangible that can be **tracked, traded,**

or rewarded. This token-based approach challenges the "user = product" paradigm of Web2, where platforms profit from user data and ad targeting. Instead, tokens enable users to capture a portion of the value they help create, reshaping how we think about ownership and incentives in digital communities.

3.3 Smart Contracts

One of the most transformative inventions tied to blockchain technology is the concept of the **smart contract**. Originally coined by computer scientist Nick Szabo in the 1990s, a smart contract is often described as **self-executing code** that runs on a blockchain. Once certain conditions are met, the smart contract carries out its instructions automatically, without requiring further human intervention. This radically changes how agreements or transactions can be handled online.

From Legal Contracts to Code

In the traditional world, contracts are written in legal language and rely on enforcement by courts or arbitration if one party fails to uphold their end of the agreement. Smart contracts, however, are **digital protocols** that enforce their own rules. If the code says, "When Person A sends 1 Ether, Person B will release Ownership Document X," the exchange happens automatically once Person A sends that Ether to the specified address. There's no need for a lawyer or escrow service to confirm that both parties acted in good faith; the **blockchain network** itself enforces the logic.

Core Properties of Smart Contracts

1. **Autonomy**: Once deployed to the blockchain, a smart contract executes its terms without requiring an intermediary like a bank, lawyer, or other middleman.

2. **Trustless Execution**: The integrity of a smart contract's actions is guaranteed by the blockchain's consensus mechanism. Users

can trust the code because it's publicly visible (on open blockchains) and tamper-resistant.

3. **Transparency**: Anyone can inspect the code of a public smart contract to verify what it does. This transparency fosters trust in decentralized applications.

4. **Irreversibility**: Actions carried out by a smart contract are typically irreversible once confirmed. This property demands caution in coding; mistakes in a contract's logic can lead to unintended consequences or lost funds.

How Smart Contracts Are Deployed

Developers write smart contracts in specialized programming languages tailored to specific blockchains. For example:

- **Solidity**: The most common language for writing smart contracts on Ethereum.

- **Vyper**: A Python-like language also used on Ethereum, focusing on simplicity and security.

- **Rust**: Used by blockchains like Solana, NEAR, and Polkadot for building high-performance contracts.

After coding, the developer compiles the contract into bytecode and deploys it on the blockchain, paying a network fee (often called "gas" on Ethereum) to cover the computational cost of adding the contract to the ledger.

Real-World Applications

1. **Decentralized Finance (DeFi)**: Smart contracts enable lending, borrowing, trading, and yield farming without banks or brokers. For example, protocols like Aave or Compound let users deposit crypto assets and earn interest or take out collateralized loans.

2. **Token Creation and Management**: As noted earlier, ERC-20 and ERC-721 tokens are governed by smart contracts that define supply, transfer rules, and ownership tracking.

3. **Escrow and Arbitration**: Smart contracts can act as digital escrows, releasing funds only after certain conditions (like delivery confirmation) are met. Some platforms include arbitration modules that allow a trusted third party to intervene if there's a dispute.

4. **Supply Chain Tracking**: By pairing IoT devices with smart contracts, companies can track the journey of goods from production to delivery in a transparent, tamper-proof way.

Oracles and Off-Chain Data

Smart contracts can only access data already on the blockchain, which poses a limitation for many real-world applications. Enter the concept of **oracles**—services or systems that feed external data into the blockchain. For example, a weather oracle might provide temperature data so that a parametric insurance smart contract can automatically pay farmers if temperatures dip below a threshold. Oracles thus act as bridges between on-chain code and off-chain reality, expanding the potential use cases of smart contracts.

Security Considerations

Because smart contracts hold and manage real economic value, they attract hackers. **Bugs, exploits, or logical flaws** in the code can lead to losses in the millions or even billions of dollars. Projects often hire specialized auditing firms to review their contracts before deployment. Additionally, decentralized insurance solutions have emerged to protect users from catastrophic smart contract failures.

Limitations and Future Directions

- **Complexity**: Writing bug-free smart contracts is challenging. Human error can have significant consequences.

- **Scalability**: Popular blockchains like Ethereum have faced congestion issues. Layer-2 solutions (e.g., Optimistic Rollups, zkRollups) and alternative blockchains aim to solve this.

- **Legal Uncertainty**: While code-as-law is compelling, smart contracts still operate in a legal gray area. Courts may or may not recognize their outcomes as binding if real-world disputes arise.

In the bigger Web3 picture, smart contracts are indispensable. They enable decentralized governance, automated financial services, and trustless interactions. As the technology matures, we can expect smart contracts to play an ever-larger role in everything from decentralized social media platforms to automated supply chain management and beyond.

3.4 Decentralized Apps (dApps) and Protocols

With blockchains providing the infrastructure, tokens offering value exchange, and smart contracts automating logic, we arrive at the final cornerstone: **decentralized applications (dApps)** and protocols. These are the practical, user-facing or developer-facing tools that harness the above components to deliver real-world services—ranging from financial products and marketplaces to social media and identity systems.

What Are dApps?

A **decentralized application (dApp)** is an application whose back-end code runs on a decentralized network rather than a single server. This typically involves:

1. **Smart Contracts**: Deployed on a

blockchain like Ethereum, Solana, or BNB Chain.

2. **Front-End**: Often a web or mobile interface that interacts with the blockchain through a wallet or other integration.

3. **Decentralized Storage**: For large files, dApps may use systems like IPFS (InterPlanetary File System) or Arweave to store data off-chain while keeping references on-chain.

What distinguishes a dApp from a standard web application is the reliance on **open protocols** and a consensus-driven state machine (the blockchain). Traditional apps rely on private servers that belong to a single company, whereas dApps distribute trust among multiple nodes. This eliminates single points of failure or control, offering a **censorship-resistant** and more user-sovereign experience.

Evolution of Decentralized Protocols

Before the term "dApp" became popular, blockchain projects were already developing **protocols**—formal rules and standards for network operations. For instance, the **Bitcoin protocol** dictates how nodes propagate transactions, how miners propose blocks, and how consensus is achieved. Ethereum extended these ideas, letting developers build new protocols on top of the base layer for token creation, decentralized finance, and more.

A **protocol** is not the same as an app. Rather, it's a set of rules and data structures that multiple parties can adopt. Once a protocol is established, developers can create many dApps using that standard. For example, the **ERC-20** standard is a protocol for fungible tokens on Ethereum. Countless dApps and wallets support ERC-20 tokens because they follow the same interface.

Categories of dApps

1. **Decentralized Finance (DeFi)**: Includes

protocols for lending, borrowing, trading, yield farming, stablecoins, and more. Examples: Uniswap, MakerDAO, Aave.

2. **NFT Marketplaces and Art Platforms**: Allow creators to mint, buy, and sell non-fungible tokens. Examples: OpenSea, Rarible, Foundation.

3. **Gaming and Metaverse**: Focus on in-game assets as NFTs and digital real estate, enabling "play-to-earn" economies. Examples: Axie Infinity, The Sandbox, Decentraland.

4. **Social and Content Platforms**: Attempt to reinvent social media, blogging, or video sharing in a decentralized manner, often rewarding creators with tokens. Examples: Lens Protocol, Mirror.xyz.

5. **Identity and Reputation**: Provide self-sovereign identity solutions that let individuals control their personal data and

reputation without relying on big tech logins. Examples: ENS (Ethereum Name Service), BrightID, Ceramic Network.

Benefits of dApps

1. **User Sovereignty**: Data is not stored on a central server that can be shut down or mined for profit by a corporation.

2. **Censorship Resistance**: As long as the blockchain and distributed storage system remain operational, no single party can unilaterally remove or block content.

3. **Interoperability**: Many dApps running on the same blockchain can easily integrate. For instance, a DeFi platform can use an NFT as collateral if they both adhere to the same token standards.

4. **Innovation and Open Source**: The open nature of most dApps encourages collaboration and rapid iteration.

Developers can fork existing code or build on top of existing protocols.

Challenges Facing dApps

- **User Experience**: Interacting with blockchain networks can still be cumbersome (e.g., needing a wallet, paying gas fees, handling private keys). Improving ease of use remains a core challenge.

- **Scalability**: Blockchains can become congested, leading to high fees or slow confirmation times. Layer-2 solutions and next-generation blockchains aim to address this.

- **Regulatory Hurdles**: Some dApps, especially those dealing with finance, may face legal scrutiny or require compliance with anti-money laundering (AML) and know-your-customer (KYC) regulations.

- **Security**: A single bug in a smart contract

can compromise the entire dApp, potentially leading to large-scale losses.

- **Onboarding Mainstream Users**: Familiarizing casual users with seed phrases, gas fees, and decentralized governance can be difficult.

Protocol Layer vs. Application Layer

It's important to differentiate between the **protocol layer** and the **application layer** in the Web3 stack:

- **Protocol Layer**: Provides base functionality or standards for how certain actions take place (e.g., transferring tokens, verifying identity, or launching a DAO). Protocols are often run or maintained by decentralized communities through governance tokens.

- **Application Layer**: The user-facing part— websites or mobile apps that call on these protocols. For instance, multiple wallet apps might all leverage the same DeFi protocol but present different user interfaces and features.

This modular design fosters a vibrant ecosystem where **composable** applications can quickly integrate with each other. For example, a user's NFT minted on one marketplace can be listed on another, or used as collateral in a DeFi platform, if they share the same token standard.

Notable Examples of dApps and Protocols

- **Uniswap**: A decentralized exchange (DEX) protocol on Ethereum enabling automated token swaps without an order book.

- **Compound**: A lending protocol where users can deposit crypto assets to earn interest or borrow against collateral.

- **ENS (Ethereum Name Service)**: A protocol that lets users map complex blockchain addresses to human-readable names (like "alice.eth").

- **Filecoin/IPFS**: Protocols for decentralized file storage, allowing users to rent out hard drive space and earn tokens.

- **Arweave**: A protocol focused on permanent, tamper-proof data storage.

- **Lens Protocol**: A decentralized social media protocol that aims to let users own their social graph and content, enabling new forms of social networking across multiple dApps.

A Glimpse into the Future

As scaling solutions mature and more user-friendly interfaces emerge, the distinction between a "regular app" and a "decentralized app" may blur. Future users might not even realize they're interacting with a blockchain or paying gas fees; these complexities could be abstracted away.

Meanwhile, protocols will continue to refine governance models—like **DAOs**—to ensure that communities can effectively steer the development of their underlying platforms.

In essence, dApps and decentralized protocols stand at the frontier of what Web3 can offer: an internet that is not just user-generated (like Web2), but **user-owned and user-governed**. This paves the way for new business models, innovative forms of organization, and a reimagined relationship between platforms, creators, and end users.

Conclusion: How These Components Interact to Form Web3

Bringing all four pillars together—blockchain, tokens, smart contracts, and dApps/protocols—reveals a **self-reinforcing ecosystem**:

1. **Blockchain** provides the **infrastructure**

and **ledger** for trustless interactions.

2. **Tokens** function as units of **value**, **membership**, or **utility**, enabling new economic and governance models.

3. **Smart Contracts** automate and enforce agreements, **removing** the need for traditional intermediaries.

4. **dApps and Protocols** build on top of these foundations to **deliver** real-world applications—from decentralized finance and gaming to social media and identity services.

This interconnected web has the potential to **redefine** how value, ownership, and governance work online. Instead of relying on centralized tech giants or financial institutions, users can transact, create, and collaborate **directly**, supported by code that executes transparently and autonomously. It's a world in which **communities** can govern themselves via tokens and smart contracts, and where data can live on networks that no single authority can unilaterally control or censor.

The Road Ahead

Despite its promise, Web3 is still in its **early stages**, wrestling with issues of scalability, user experience, regulation, and security. Critics argue that many current projects fail to live up to the ideals of full decentralization and user sovereignty, pointing to reliance on centralized platforms for on-ramps and off-ramps. Others note that speculation often overshadows genuine innovation, as hype-driven markets can overshadow serious development.

Yet, the core **technological breakthroughs**—blockchain as a decentralized database, tokens for on-chain economics, smart contracts for automated trust, and dApps for censorship-resistant applications—have **lasting significance**. Developers around the globe are working tirelessly to solve the challenges and build intuitive, scalable solutions that could one day make Web3 the new normal for internet interactions.

Why It All Matters

- **Empowerment**: Web3 tools empower individuals to own their digital assets, identities, and communities.

- **Innovation**: Developers can create applications that are composable, interoperable, and not locked behind proprietary APIs or walled gardens.

- **Resilience**: A decentralized network is more resistant to single points of failure and censorship.

- **Inclusion**: Anyone with an internet connection can participate, potentially reducing barriers to entry and fostering global collaboration.

By understanding these four key building blocks, you gain an insider's view of where the internet might be heading—and how you can participate in shaping that future. Whether you're a casual user intrigued by decentralized finance, a business owner exploring new ways to engage customers, or an artist looking to tokenize your creations, the **foundation** of Web3 is built to support you in ways that the centralized Web2 simply cannot.

Ultimately, **Web3** represents a shift from platforms to **protocols**, from shareholders to **stakeholders**, and from user data exploitation to **user data empowerment**. As these foundational technologies mature, we may witness the emergence of a truly global, user-centric digital ecosystem—fulfilling the internet's original promise of open, inclusive, and collaborative innovation on a scale we have only begun to imagine.

Chapter 4: Decentralized Identity

The internet has dramatically transformed how we interact, conduct business, and share information. Yet, one aspect remains surprisingly archaic: **how we manage our identities online**. Today's mainstream identity solutions rely on centralized servers owned by large corporations or government authorities. Whether it's logging into your favorite social media platform using an email and password, or proving your age by uploading a state-issued ID, the control over your digital existence typically lies outside your own hands.

This structural imbalance is at the heart of today's pressing concerns about data privacy, surveillance capitalism, and user autonomy. Against this backdrop, **decentralized identity**—sometimes called **self-sovereign identity**—emerges as a key component of Web3's mission to create a more user-centric internet. By leveraging cryptography, distributed ledgers, and user-owned data vaults, decentralized identity systems hold the promise of putting you, the user, back in the driver's seat of your online persona.

4.1 What Is Decentralized Identity?

The Problem with Traditional, Centralized Identity

For most people, verifying who they are online relies on third parties. When you sign up for a new website, you might connect via Google or Facebook credentials (the classic "Log in with Google/Facebook" button) or create a username/password combination. In each case:

1. **A Centralized Database**: Your account data is typically stored on the service provider's servers, granting them broad

control over your identity.

2. **Single Points of Failure**: If the service experiences a data breach, hackers gain access to your account details—or worse, your personal information, which can lead to identity theft.

3. **Cross-Service Tracking**: Large identity providers (e.g., Google, Facebook) can correlate your activities across different platforms, building extensive profiles on your behavior.

4. **Limited User Autonomy**: If a platform suspends your account or goes out of business, you may lose access to all your data and contacts tied to that account.

While these traditional methods have simplified account creation and user onboarding, they've also led to widespread privacy concerns and a lack of user sovereignty. You're effectively forced to trust service providers to protect your sensitive information and respect your privacy—often, that trust is broken or misused.

Defining Decentralized Identity

Decentralized identity flips this model upside down. Instead of handing over your data to each website or service, you store your identity attributes and credentials in a system that **you** control, typically using cryptographic keys and blockchain-based or distributed data storage. Then, when a website needs to verify you—whether you're old enough to buy a product or hold a valid membership in a certain organization—you can choose precisely what information to share.

This approach is sometimes called **self-sovereign identity (SSI)** because the individual, rather than a centralized authority, wields ultimate control over the credentials. The core principles include:

1. **User-Controlled Data**: You decide who gets to see your credentials, and you can revoke access at any time.

2. **Portability**: Your identity is not locked to a single platform; you can carry it across websites, apps, and even offline scenarios (like proving membership at an event).

3. **Selective Disclosure**: Through advanced cryptography (like zero-knowledge proofs), you can prove facts about yourself without revealing unnecessary personal details.

4. **Minimized Trust**: You don't have to rely on one corporation or government entity to store and validate your identity; trust is distributed across a network.

Key Terms: Decentralized Identifiers (DIDs) and Verifiable Credentials

Two concepts often come up in discussions about decentralized identity:

- **Decentralized Identifiers (DIDs)**: These are unique identifiers (like "did:example:12345abcde") that point to a

DID document on a distributed ledger or other decentralized network. Unlike email addresses or usernames, DIDs aren't controlled by any single authority. They're designed to be resolvable and persistent, meaning they can exist as long as the owner wishes and can be used across multiple services.

- **Verifiable Credentials (VCs)**: These are tamper-proof, cryptographically signed statements about an identity. For example, a university could issue a verifiable credential stating you have a bachelor's degree. You store this credential in your digital wallet. Later, you can present a proof to a prospective employer without revealing sensitive info like your entire transcript or student ID.

The **World Wide Web Consortium (W3C)** has been instrumental in standardizing these concepts, ensuring that different decentralized identity solutions can interoperate. The overarching goal is an internet in which people, organizations, and even things (like IoT devices) can securely share credentials without needing large centralized intermediaries.

Why Decentralized Identity Matters

Decentralized identity addresses a range of pain points in our current digital landscape:

1. **Privacy**: By only sharing the credentials or data points necessary for a transaction or verification, you reduce the risk of data leaks.

2. **Security**: Because credentials are verified with cryptographic signatures, it's harder for bad actors to forge or tamper with them.

3. **Inclusion**: In parts of the world where citizens don't have easy access to government ID, a decentralized approach can provide a portable, verifiable means of

identity.

4. **User Empowerment**: You can pick and choose which credentials to reveal, and you can do so without relying on a major tech company or government controlling the entire process.

It's important to note that the concept is still evolving. Many decentralized identity solutions are in pilot stages or early adoption phases, and challenges remain—interoperability across ecosystems, user experience complexity, and regulatory acceptance, to name a few. Yet, the momentum is strong, with multiple startups, nonprofits, and even major corporations and governments exploring ways to make decentralized identity mainstream.

The Road Ahead

Decentralized identity might eventually transform everything from how we log into our favorite apps to how we prove our citizenship. It could also blend seamlessly with other aspects of Web3, like decentralized finance (DeFi) and token-based communities, creating a world where you can join a DAO (Decentralized Autonomous Organization) and vote on proposals without revealing your entire real-world identity—just enough proof that you're an eligible member.

In the sections that follow, we'll dive deeper into **digital wallets and keys**—the core tools you use to manage a decentralized identity—and explore **how ownership of personal data** shifts in this paradigm. Finally, we'll look at **potential uses and everyday benefits**, showing how decentralized identity can solve real-world problems and empower users in ways that centralized identity models cannot.

4.2 Digital Wallets and Keys

The Foundation of Decentralized Identity

If decentralized identity is about giving you full control over your online persona, then **digital wallets** and **cryptographic keys** are the tools that make this control possible. Think of these wallets as more than just places to store cryptocurrencies. In the context of decentralized identity, a digital wallet becomes **your personal vault** for identity documents, credentials, and other proofs.

Unlike a password manager or an email account, your digital wallet doesn't rely on a central server that can be hacked or taken offline. Instead, it leverages cryptographic techniques to store your private keys safely and facilitate secure interactions on decentralized networks. This architecture is crucial for guaranteeing authenticity, preventing tampering, and ensuring only you can access or share your data.

Public and Private Keys: The Heart of Cryptography

At the core of any decentralized identity system are **cryptographic keys**—a public key and a corresponding private key:

- **Public Key**: As the name suggests, this can be safely shared with anyone. It's often used to verify digital signatures or to encrypt data intended for you. Think of it like your mailbox address—you need to share it so people can send you letters, but it doesn't let them open your mailbox.

- **Private Key**: This must **never** be shared. It's the secret that allows you to create digital signatures or decrypt messages intended for you. It's akin to having the only key that can open your mailbox. In decentralized identity, your private key essentially proves you are the legitimate owner of a particular DID or set of credentials.

Wallet Structures and UI

Digital wallets come in different forms:

1. **Software Wallets**: These might be mobile or desktop apps, like MetaMask, Phantom, or dedicated identity wallets from SSI-focused companies. They're convenient for everyday use but can be vulnerable to malware or hacking if not properly secured.

2. **Hardware Wallets**: Physical devices that store your private keys offline (e.g., Ledger, Trezor). They're less vulnerable to online hacks, but you have to keep the device safe from physical theft or damage.

3. **Smart Contract Wallets**: A more advanced type of wallet, these can incorporate "account abstraction," meaning features like multi-signature control, spending limits, or social recovery (in case you lose your device). They exist as smart contracts on certain blockchains (e.g., Ethereum), combining convenience with security.

While these wallets initially gained popularity for managing cryptocurrencies, the same cryptographic mechanisms can secure any data or credentials you wish to protect—including your decentralized identity attributes.

User Experience Challenges

One of the biggest hurdles to widespread adoption of decentralized identity is **usability**. Managing a digital wallet with cryptographic keys can be intimidating:

- **Private Key Storage**: You're responsible for securely storing "seed phrases" (12–24 words that back up your wallet) or other recovery methods. If you lose your seed phrase, you could lose access to your identity and assets forever.

- **Complex Interfaces**: Many crypto wallets today use interfaces built primarily for tokens, not identity credentials. Users need a straightforward way to store and present verifiable credentials without confusion.

- **Recovery Mechanisms**: What happens if you forget your password or lose access to your device? Traditional identity solutions often have a "Forgot Password?" button, but in decentralized systems, you can't just call up a help desk—your data is truly under your control.

Innovations like **social recovery** (where multiple trusted contacts can collectively help you regain access) or **multi-factor authentication** using biometric or hardware keys are emerging to address these concerns. The challenge is to balance strong security with user-friendly design.

Wallet Interoperability

Ideally, a decentralized identity wallet shouldn't lock you into a single blockchain or ecosystem. In reality, many wallets focus on specific blockchains or token standards. This fragmentation can create confusion. Standardization efforts—like the **W3C**

DID and **Verifiable Credential** specifications—aim to ensure that no matter which wallet you use, you can present and verify credentials across multiple systems.

This interoperability is critical to realize the vision of a self-sovereign identity that truly belongs to you, not to a corporate silo or a single blockchain platform.

Keys as the Gatekeepers of Identity

When you use a decentralized identity wallet, you might:

1. **Generate or Import a DID**: This is your unique identifier.

2. **Receive Verifiable Credentials**: These could be diplomas, membership badges, licenses, etc. Each credential is cryptographically signed by the issuer's private key, so anyone can verify authenticity using the issuer's public key.

3. **Selective Disclosure**: When proving something—like your age or membership status—you show only the minimal data required. You sign this presentation with your private key, ensuring it can't be forged by anyone else.

In each transaction, your private key underlies your authority to act as the owner of the DID or credentials. If a malicious entity somehow obtains your private key, they can impersonate you or manipulate your data. That's why secure key management is crucial.

The Future of Wallets for Identity

We're moving toward a future where a digital wallet might store everything from your passport data and driver's license to your professional certifications and social media reputation scores. Already, experiments are underway:

- **State-Issued IDs on Blockchain**: Some regions are piloting digital driver's licenses or national ID programs secured via decentralized solutions.

- **Healthcare Credentials**: Immunization or health records, verifiably stored in your wallet and presented on demand.

- **Enterprise Access Management**: Companies exploring how employees can log into internal systems using self-sovereign credentials rather than centralized corporate directories.

As these use cases mature, the concept of a "wallet" as a multi-purpose identity manager will likely become mainstream. You'll authenticate to websites, prove membership, sign documents, and even encrypt messages, all using the same cryptographic keys—**your** keys.

Yet with great power comes great responsibility. The convenience of a self-sovereign identity depends on each user's ability (and willingness) to learn how to manage cryptographic keys safely. For many, that will require a shift in mindset—from relying on tech giants or IT departments to taking personal ownership of one's digital life.

4.3 Ownership of Personal Data

The Status Quo: Data Monopolies

In the **Web2** era, personal data ownership is murky at best. When you post photos, comments, or personal details on a social media platform, the terms of service often grant the platform broad rights to store, analyze, and even sell aggregated insights about you to advertisers. This arrangement has fueled the rise of "data monopolies," where a handful of companies accumulate vast troves of user information, from demographic details to real-time location data.

This centralized data model has serious drawbacks:

1. **Privacy Violations**: High-profile scandals (e.g., Cambridge Analytica) demonstrate

how user data can be misused to manipulate public opinion.

2. **Breach Vulnerabilities**: A single data breach can compromise millions—sometimes billions—of personal records at once.

3. **Opaque Data Practices**: Users rarely know precisely what data is collected, how it's used, or how to control it.

4. **Lack of User Autonomy**: If you decide to leave a platform, you often can't take your data with you in any meaningful way.

Data Ownership in Decentralized Identity

In contrast, **decentralized identity** frameworks take a radically different approach to data. Instead of storing personal information in a centralized server, the data is either:

- **Stored Locally**: On your own device or private storage, encrypted and only accessible by you.

- **Stored in Decentralized Storage**: For larger datasets, solutions like IPFS, Arweave, or Filecoin provide distributed storage, but the encryption keys and access controls remain in your hands.

- **Verifiable Credentials**: Rather than handing over raw data to each service, you show cryptographic proofs. For example, if you need to prove you're over 18, you can present a zero-knowledge proof that verifies this fact without revealing your exact birth date.

Because you control the keys to your identity wallet, you inherently control your data. You decide which services can view or copy your credentials. If you revoke access, they no longer can validate or see those credentials unless they cache them locally—but even then, the validity can be made to expire. This shift puts you at the center of the data ownership equation.

Minimizing Data Footprints

Decentralized identity systems often encourage a principle called **data minimization**. Instead of collecting every bit of information about a user, a service only asks for what's strictly necessary. This might mean:

- **Proof of Age** instead of a full birth date.

- **Proof of Location** instead of your complete address.

- **Proof of Skill/Certification** instead of your entire resume.

Cryptographic techniques such as **zero-knowledge proofs** (ZKPs) enable these selective disclosures. For instance, a ZKP can allow you to prove you're older than 18 without revealing your date of birth. Or you can prove you have a valid driver's license without exposing the license number or your home address. This approach not only enhances privacy but also significantly reduces the risk of identity theft or data leaks.

Challenges to Data Ownership

Achieving true data ownership in practice faces several obstacles:

1. **Regulatory Uncertainty**: Governments worldwide have varied data protection laws. How do decentralized systems comply with regulations like GDPR (Right to be Forgotten) if data is stored on immutable ledgers? Creative approaches like encrypting the data off-chain and only storing references on-chain can help, but there's still legal ambiguity.

2. **User Responsibility**: Holding your own data means you must secure it. Not everyone has the technical literacy to manage encryption keys or recovery mechanisms. A "lost" key could mean losing vital records.

3. **Adoption Barriers**: Many services rely on monetizing user data. Shifting to a user-centric model requires rethinking business strategies. Will platforms offer paid tiers instead of free, ad-driven models? Or might tokenized incentives replace advertising revenue?

The Economics of User-Owned Data

One intriguing possibility is that user-owned data could become a negotiable asset. In a Web3 marketplace, you might choose to **opt-in** to share certain data points with a marketer in exchange for tokens or other rewards. Instead of platforms unilaterally profiting from your data, you'd receive a share of the value generated. This concept resonates with the broader ethos of **fair data marketplaces** and could redefine the relationship between users, advertisers, and developers.

However, critics argue this could create a "data capitalism" scenario where people commodify deeply personal information for short-term gain. Balancing privacy with economic incentives remains an open question. Still, the potential for more equitable data economies is real.

Real-World Examples

- **Health Records**: In some pilot projects, patients store their medical data in decentralized vaults, granting doctors or hospitals temporary access. After treatment, that access is revoked.

- **Educational Credentials**: Universities issue verifiable digital diplomas directly to students, who can share them with employers or scholarship programs. The students, not the institutions, control who sees the credentials.

- **Job Market Platforms**: Instead of uploading your resume to a centralized jobs site, you store your verifiable work history in your wallet. When applying for a job, you share relevant credentials, and once the interview process is over, you can revoke them.

These experiments demonstrate a fundamental change: data about you, once minted as a credential, belongs to **you**, not a corporate database.

A Paradigm Shift

Decentralized identity and data ownership can be seen as part of a broader **paradigm shift** toward user autonomy and dignity in the digital realm. Instead of scattering personal data across countless servers, you hold it in a secure, unified place, revealing only what you must. This shift from "company owns your data" to "you own your data" aligns with the movement to create a more **ethical, privacy-preserving** internet.

Of course, this vision is not yet fully realized. Many technical, legal, and cultural hurdles must be cleared to make decentralized data ownership the norm rather than the exception. But the direction is clear: if Web3 aspires to disrupt centralized power structures and empower individuals, **owning your personal data** is a central pillar of that revolution.

4.4 Potential Uses and Everyday Benefits

Moving Beyond Abstract Concepts

Thus far, we've discussed the philosophical and technical underpinnings of decentralized identity: self-sovereign ownership of credentials, cryptographic wallets, and selective disclosure of data. But how does this translate into real-world utility? Where do we see tangible benefits that might convince average users, businesses, and organizations to adopt a new way of managing identity?

In this section, we'll explore a range of **use cases**—from routine logins to global humanitarian efforts—

and illustrate how decentralized identity is already providing solutions to age-old problems of trust, privacy, and data management.

1. Seamless and Secure Logins

Traditional Approach: Creating yet another username and password for each website. Or "logging in with Google/Facebook," thereby sharing your data with third-party platforms.

Decentralized Identity Approach: Instead of multiple passwords, you use your cryptographic wallet or identity manager to authenticate. The website doesn't store your personal details—it verifies your DID-based credentials. This can reduce password fatigue, risk of credential stuffing attacks, and centralized data breaches.

- **Benefit**: Enhanced security, single-point control of your identity, minimized data shared with websites.

- **Example**: Logging into a social media

platform using your DID means you own your contacts and content—if you move to another platform, you can take your social graph with you, as long as it's stored under your personal control.

2. Proof of Age or Residency Without Oversharing

Traditional Approach: Showing a physical ID card (with full name, address, photo, birth date) even if you only need to prove you're over 18 or a resident of a certain region.

Decentralized Identity Approach: Present a **verifiable credential** or zero-knowledge proof that confirms you meet the criteria—without revealing unnecessary personal details. If you need to prove residency, you display a digitally signed credential from a government or utility provider attesting to your region.

- **Benefit**: Privacy preservation, reduced risk of identity theft, streamlined verification for online or in-person services.

- **Example**: Purchasing age-restricted products online or verifying local residency to access community resources (e.g., local library e-books).

3. Verifiable Credentials in Education and Employment

Traditional Approach: Institutions issue paper degrees or credentials that can be lost, forged, or require tedious background checks. Potential employers often wait weeks to verify transcripts.

Decentralized Identity Approach: Educational institutions can issue **verifiable credentials** directly to students' wallets. Employers can confirm authenticity instantly by checking the issuer's public key on a blockchain or distributed ledger.

- **Benefit**: Quick, global verification of qualifications, reduced administrative overhead, and near-elimination of credential fraud.

- **Example**: A job candidate applies to a global tech firm. Rather than manually uploading PDFs of diplomas, they share cryptographic proofs that their degrees and certifications are genuine.

4. Healthcare and Medical Records

Traditional Approach: Patient data is siloed within each hospital, clinic, or insurance provider. Transferring records can be slow, and patients often have minimal control over who sees them.

Decentralized Identity Approach: You hold your medical history in an encrypted data store linked to your DID. Healthcare providers can request access, which you grant temporarily. Following treatment, you can revoke access, ensuring ongoing privacy.

- **Benefit**: Improved patient autonomy, streamlined record-sharing across providers, lower likelihood of medical identity theft.

- **Example**: Traveling abroad and needing urgent care? You can grant a foreign clinic temporary, verifiable access to your relevant health records without sending them unencrypted emails or faxes.

5. Humanitarian and Global Identity Solutions

Traditional Approach: In many regions, especially war-torn or disaster-affected areas, official ID documents can be lost or destroyed. Refugees may struggle to prove who they are, complicating aid distribution or resettlement processes.

Decentralized Identity Approach: By issuing digital identities via humanitarian organizations or recognized nonprofits, displaced individuals can maintain credentials attesting to who they are, their family relationships, or their professional qualifications. They don't rely on a government registry that may no longer exist or be accessible.

- **Benefit**: Preservation of identity even under extreme circumstances, easier cross-border coordination of aid, and protection against identity fraud in vulnerable populations.

- **Example**: An international NGO sets up a system where refugees store verifiable ID credentials on their phones. As they move between camps or countries, local authorities can validate their status instantly.

6. Token-Gated Communities and Event Access

Traditional Approach: Printed or digital tickets for events, which can be resold multiple times or counterfeited. Online communities often rely on basic password-protected forums or subscription models, which can be shared without permission.

Decentralized Identity Approach: The event or community can issue a **token** or **verifiable credential** granting access. Your digital wallet proves you're an authorized attendee or community member. Once the credential expires, you can't reuse it or transfer it without permission (if it's non-transferable).

- **Benefit**: Enhanced security against counterfeit tickets, direct relationship between organizers and participants, frictionless membership management.

- **Example**: A music festival issues NFT tickets that double as collectible art. Scanners at the gates verify the NFT's authenticity on the blockchain, reducing ticket fraud.

7. IoT and Device Identity

Traditional Approach: IoT devices rely on hard-coded credentials or manufacturer servers to verify their legitimacy. Hacking vulnerabilities abound when centralized servers store thousands of device credentials.

Decentralized Identity Approach: Each IoT device can register its own DID and maintain credentials securely. Firmware updates or data transmissions are cryptographically signed, ensuring no tampering or spoofing. The user or device owner, not the manufacturer, ultimately controls how the device is used or what data it shares.

- **Benefit**: Reduced single points of failure, easier device onboarding, tamper-proof logs of device history (e.g., for maintenance).

- **Example**: A smart lock that only grants access if the requesting person's DID-based credential matches specific conditions (time of day, membership in the homeowner's family group).

Everyday Benefits and Shifting the Power Dynamic

Beyond these discrete use cases, decentralized identity encourages a **fundamental rebalancing of power**:

- **Individual Empowerment**: You gain control over how your identity is used and monetized, rather than platforms profiting from your data.

- **Reduced Data Breach Impact**: Even if a service is compromised, your sensitive details aren't stored on their servers.

- **Interoperability and Portability**: Credentials you acquire in one context can seamlessly apply to others, saving time and paperwork.

- **Innovation and Competition**: Startups can build new services that rely on user-owned identity data without having to first capture that data themselves, fostering open ecosystems.

Overcoming Adoption Barriers

For decentralized identity to deliver these everyday benefits, a few hurdles must be addressed:

1. **User Education**: People need to understand why decentralized identity is safer, how to manage private keys, and when to use verifiable credentials.

2. **Regulatory Clarity**: Governments must figure out how to recognize DID-based credentials. Some forward-thinking locales already do, but mass adoption requires broader legal frameworks.

3. **Business Models**: Many current Web2 platforms rely on ad revenue derived from user data. Decentralized identity disrupts this. Will new models—like subscription fees, token economies, or data marketplaces—take hold?

4. **Technical Standardization**: Cross-chain

and cross-ecosystem compatibility remains a challenge. More robust standards will smooth friction and open up synergy between platforms.

Despite these challenges, the **trend line** is clear: more organizations, governments, and users are recognizing the value of user-controlled identity. As these systems mature, decentralized identity could become as ubiquitous and effortless as email sign-ups—only this time, you won't be handing over your personal data to a central authority. Instead, you'll be engaging in a more privacy-preserving, transparent, and **truly user-centric** digital world.

Conclusion

Decentralized identity stands at the nexus of trust, privacy, and user empowerment in the evolving Web3 landscape. It challenges the status quo of centralized logins, data monopolies, and forced reliance on tech giants or government bureaus to manage our digital personas. By harnessing **cryptographic keys**, **DIDs**, and **verifiable credentials**, individuals can claim unprecedented control over who they are online—disclosing only the minimal information needed for any given context.

Throughout this chapter, we've unpacked the foundational elements that compose decentralized identity:

- **What Is Decentralized Identity?**: A departure from centralized data silos, giving users cryptographic control over their credentials, leveraging global standards like DIDs and verifiable credentials.

- **Digital Wallets and Keys**: The mechanism for storing private keys, managing self-sovereign identities, and enabling secure authentication.

- **Ownership of Personal Data**: A paradigm shift away from corporate servers toward user-owned, encrypted repositories, enabling selective disclosure via zero-knowledge proofs and other privacy-preserving tools.

- **Potential Uses and Everyday Benefits**: From frictionless logins and portable educational records to safer healthcare data and humanitarian ID solutions, decentralized identity has wide-ranging real-world applications.

Of course, the journey is not without **challenges**. Questions persist around user experience, recovery mechanisms, regulatory frameworks, and scaling these solutions to billions of people. But the momentum behind decentralized identity is strong, driven by the converging forces of blockchain innovation, user privacy demands, and the need for more resilient global infrastructures.

As Web3 continues to evolve, decentralized identity will likely be a linchpin: enabling new forms of online collaboration, commerce, and governance that respect individual autonomy and minimize data risks. Whether you're a curious internet user, a policy maker, or a developer, understanding decentralized identity is key to appreciating the broader promise of a more democratic, user-owned web. By placing **you** in charge of your data, your credentials, and your online self, this emerging technology paves the way for a future where digital interactions reflect genuine trust, consent, and freedom.

Chapter 5: Token-Based Communities

The term "token" often conjures up images of cryptocurrency markets, Bitcoin price charts, and day traders buying and selling digital assets for profit. While **financial speculation** on tokens is undeniably a big part of the crypto world, an equally powerful—and in many ways more exciting—realm exists where tokens are used to build and enhance communities.

Before we dive in, let's clarify what we mean by **token-based communities**. Essentially, these are groups of people who use a shared digital token (or multiple tokens) to coordinate activities, reward contributions, and govern decisions. Imagine a neighborhood co-op, a sports fan club, or a social media group where each member holds a special "badge" or "pass" that grants them certain privileges—except that, in Web3, these badges are recorded on a blockchain as **tokens**. They can represent anything from membership rights and voting power to exclusive perks or content access.

These communities can span everything from local grassroots groups to global internet tribes, and they're rapidly gaining traction because tokens introduce a sense of **shared ownership**. This is a major shift from Web2 platforms, where the platform owner (e.g., a social media company) typically holds all the power. In a token-based community, power is distributed among the token holders, who can influence decisions, share in the value created, and vote on the future direction of the group.

In the sections ahead, we'll explore:

1. **Understanding Tokens Beyond Money**: Tokens aren't just digital cash; they can represent social capital, governance rights, or even just "membership status."

2. **Community Tokens and Social Tokens**: How groups, creators, and

influencers use custom tokens to build stronger bonds and reward loyalty.

3. **DAOs (Decentralized Autonomous Organizations) and Their Role**: The organizational structure that often underpins token-based communities, enabling transparent, collective decision-making.

4. **Real-World Examples and Use Cases**: Practical illustrations of how token-based communities operate, from artist collectives to investment clubs to social clubs.

Let's begin by exploring how we've moved beyond the idea that tokens are "just money."

5.1 Understanding Tokens Beyond Money

The Evolution of the Word "Token"

The word "token" has been around for ages—it used

to refer to small physical items you'd exchange, like a bus token or an arcade token. When blockchain technology exploded onto the scene with Bitcoin in 2009, "token" started to take on a new meaning. People began to associate tokens with digital currencies or "coins" that you could trade on crypto exchanges.

Yet, **not all tokens are created equal**. Many of them serve functions that go well beyond a currency-like role. In the Web3 space, the same underlying technology (blockchain) that powers cryptocurrencies can also power tokens representing membership rights, points in a loyalty program, or even purely symbolic badges that show you're a fan of a particular artist.

This shift from "token as money" to "token as membership or utility" is a major reason why token-based communities have become so intriguing. If you think of a token more like a **membership key**—or a digital version of a sports jersey, a backstage pass, or a stock share—then it becomes much easier to see how tokens can shape communal life.

Fungible vs. Non-Fungible Tokens

To fully grasp the concept of tokens, it's helpful to know there are two main types:

1. **Fungible Tokens (FTs)**: These tokens are **interchangeable**. One unit of a fungible token is effectively the same as another. Regular money (like dollars or euros) is fungible: any dollar bill is worth the same as any other, assuming it isn't a collectible or has a unique serial number of note. In crypto, Bitcoin or Ethereum are fungible tokens—1 ETH is always "equal" to another 1 ETH.

2. **Non-Fungible Tokens (NFTs)**: These are **unique** tokens. Each NFT has its own distinct properties. Think of them like collectible trading cards or pieces of art: one item in a series might be worth more or have

different traits than another. This uniqueness makes NFTs ideal for digital art, in-game items, or memberships that need to be individually identifiable.

Why does this distinction matter for communities? Because **fungible tokens** are typically used to represent a community's "common currency" or membership stake (everyone holds some share in the group). **NFTs**, on the other hand, might represent unique badges, achievements, or special statuses within the community. Both can exist simultaneously in a single group, each serving a different purpose.

Utility, Governance, and Other Functions

When we say tokens can go beyond money, we also need to talk about **why** they might exist. Here are a few ways tokens can be used:

- **Utility Tokens**: Grant holders the ability to perform specific actions within a platform or ecosystem. For instance, you might need a certain token to access premium features on a decentralized app.

- **Governance Tokens**: Give holders the right to vote on proposals affecting the project or community. A governance token in a community might let you cast votes on how to spend communal funds or which new rules to adopt.

- **Social Tokens**: Represent a personal or community brand, often designed to create incentives and rewards for members (more on these shortly).

- **Collectible/NFT Tokens**: Showcase unique artwork, membership cards, or in-game assets that can't be duplicated. Sometimes these function as "tickets" or "badges" proving membership or attendance.

The point is, a token can do a lot more than stand in for cash value. It can bestow **privileges,**

responsibilities, and status within an online (or offline) community.

The Importance of Shared Alignment

One reason token-based communities are so appealing is the sense of **shared alignment** they create. When members hold the same token, they have a collective interest in seeing that token's ecosystem thrive. This might mean contributing ideas, attending events, helping with marketing, or creating new content that benefits the group.

People are naturally motivated when they have **skin in the game**—and tokens provide exactly that. Instead of passively consuming content or showing up as a bystander, token holders become **active participants** in the community's success. This shift is at the heart of the phrase "community ownership," which you'll hear frequently in the Web3 space.

5.2 Community Tokens and Social Tokens

What Are "Community Tokens"?

Imagine your favorite band decided to create a digital "backstage pass" that fans could purchase or earn by participating in the band's online fan club. Holding this digital pass (a token on a blockchain) might grant you early access to tickets, exclusive content, or direct chat sessions with band members. Now apply that concept to any group—an online forum, a sports fan club, a neighborhood group, a charity, a start-up's loyal user base—and you get the idea of **community tokens**.

Community tokens can be either fungible or non-fungible, depending on the group's goals. What matters is that they represent some stake or membership in the community. Unlike a typical membership platform run by a single company, these tokens exist on a decentralized ledger. They can be traded or held in personal wallets, and often **no single entity** can unilaterally revoke them or seize control.

Social Tokens and Creator Coins

A **social token**—sometimes called a **creator coin**—is a specific type of community token that revolves around an individual personality (like a musician, a YouTuber, or a thought leader) or a small, close-knit collective. Social tokens serve as a way for creators to **monetize** and **incentivize engagement** with their fans or followers in a more direct, personal way than ads or sponsorship deals.

Examples might include:

- **A musician** launching a social token that gives fans the ability to vote on setlists, attend private virtual events, or receive a percentage of streaming royalties.

- **A fitness influencer** issuing a token that grants holders access to exclusive workout plans, live training sessions, or merchandise drops.

- **A writer** creating a tokenized reading club, where holders can discuss her works, get early access to chapters, or even vote on plot developments for her next novel.

This **direct-to-community** model bypasses traditional intermediaries. It can also create a deeper sense of connection and shared success. If a creator's popularity grows, their social token might also become more valuable or at least more in-demand, rewarding early adopters. Conversely, if the creator fails to deliver meaningful perks, token holders might lose interest (and the token's perceived value may drop).

Aligning Incentives

One reason community and social tokens are so powerful is that they **align the incentives** of the group. If you're a token holder and the group's activities succeed, the token (whether fungible or not) might gain recognition, utility, or even monetary value on secondary markets. That's not guaranteed, but the possibility encourages members to act in the collective best interest.

For creators, tokens can act as a **powerful feedback loop**—the more they engage with the community and deliver valuable content, the happier the token holders become, which in turn can attract more participants. It's a cycle fueled by genuine collaboration rather than top-down control.

Pitfalls and Considerations

It's worth noting that social tokens and community tokens can veer into speculative territory. Some people might buy them purely in the hope of flipping them for profit, which can overshadow the actual community-building goals. Additionally, there are regulatory gray areas. If a token is marketed primarily as an investment (with promises of profit), it could run afoul of securities laws in some jurisdictions.

Hence, it's crucial for community leaders or

creators to be **transparent** about what the token does—and does not—represent. For non-technical audiences, the simplest framing is often: "Our token acts like a digital pass to our community. It might have a market value, but that's not its main purpose. We're about creating a strong network of people who care about our mission."

5.3 DAOs (Decentralized Autonomous Organizations) and Their Role

What Is a DAO?

If tokens represent the **currency** (or membership pass) of a community, then **DAOs (Decentralized Autonomous Organizations)** represent the **governance** structure. Think of a DAO as an online cooperative or club that uses smart contracts (automated code on a blockchain) and tokens to make decisions collectively.

Traditionally, organizations have a hierarchy—

managers, executives, or board members who hold decision-making power. By contrast, a DAO aims to **flatten** that structure by letting token holders propose and vote on changes. Some DAOs are entirely leaderless, while others have core teams who guide the direction. But the overarching principle remains: major decisions are typically subject to a community vote, and the outcome is enforced by code whenever possible.

How DAOs Function

1. **Token-Based Voting**: DAO members (i.e., token holders) can submit or vote on proposals. Proposals might concern spending community funds, launching new projects, or making rules about membership.

2. **Shared Treasury**: Often, a DAO manages a shared pool of funds. These funds are locked in a smart contract. No single person can withdraw them unilaterally; the

community must vote.

3. **Transparency**: Because transactions happen on a blockchain, financial flows and voting results are open for anyone to audit. This stands in stark contrast to typical organizations where finances can be opaque.

4. **Smart Contracts**: The "rules" of the DAO are often encoded in smart contracts, meaning if a proposal passes with enough votes, the result (e.g., transferring tokens from the treasury) happens automatically without any middleman.

DAOs vs. Traditional Organizations

It might be helpful to compare DAOs to more familiar structures:

- **Non-Profit or Club**: Like a non-profit, a DAO can have a mission (for instance, to fund public goods or support new artists). But rather than depending on a board of directors, DAOs rely on token holder votes.

- **Start-Up with Equity**: In some ways, holding a DAO's governance token can feel like owning shares in a start-up. However, these tokens don't necessarily represent legal equity, which is where legal complexities come in. And unlike typical start-ups, day-to-day decisions might be more open to all token holders.

- **Cooperative**: A DAO most closely resembles a cooperative, where members collectively own and manage resources. The big difference is that the management tools are digital and automated wherever possible, cutting down on overhead and central points of control.

Types of DAOs

- **Protocol DAOs**: Govern a decentralized protocol (like a lending app in crypto). Token holders vote on software upgrades or parameter changes.

- **Investment/Collector DAOs**: Pool funds to invest in assets, whether they're NFTs, early-stage start-ups, or real-world collectibles (like the group that famously attempted to buy a copy of the U.S. Constitution, hence "ConstitutionDAO").

- **Social DAOs**: Focus on building a community around shared interests—music, art, activism, or simply socializing. Their treasury might fund meetups or collaborative creative projects.

- **Media DAOs**: Create or curate content, with decisions about editorial direction or revenue distribution made collectively.

Why DAOs Matter for Token-Based Communities

DAOs offer a blueprint for **collective governance**. Rather than relying on a single community manager or central figure, tokens can empower everyone in the group to have a say. This is especially important in communities that handle shared resources or want a sense of co-ownership.

Additionally, DAOs align closely with the idea of "user-owned" or "community-owned" platforms. Imagine if Facebook was governed by the people who use it, and they had a direct stake in how it evolved. That's the ideological promise behind many DAOs: turning users into stakeholders and decision-makers, not just passive consumers.

Of course, DAOs aren't utopian. They can suffer from low voter engagement, "whale" dominance (where a few large token holders sway votes), or complicated user experiences that deter newcomers. Yet, the transparency and collective nature of DAOs still represent a bold new experiment in **digital self-governance**.

5.4 Real-World Examples and Use Cases

1. Friends with Benefits (FWB)

One of the most talked-about **social DAOs** is **Friends with Benefits (FWB)**. It's a community centered around art, culture, and crypto. Members need a certain amount of $FWB tokens to join. Once inside, they gain access to exclusive channels on Discord, live events, networking opportunities, and collaborative projects.

- **Purpose**: FWB focuses on building a curated membership of creative and tech-savvy individuals who want to explore the intersection of culture and Web3.

- **Token Mechanic**: The $FWB token acts like a ticket. You must hold a specific number of tokens to maintain membership. As FWB grew in popularity, the token price rose, making membership more exclusive.

- **Benefits**: Members collaborate on art projects, music releases, and business ideas. They also hold in-person events, turning

FWB into a global, token-gated cultural club.

For non-technical audiences, FWB is a great example of how a token can do more than just represent money—it can grant entry to a vibrant, creative social circle.

2. ConstitutionDAO

ConstitutionDAO was an online collective formed in late 2021 with a mission to purchase an original copy of the U.S. Constitution at an auction. Organizers set up a DAO, and people worldwide pooled over $40 million worth of crypto to bid.

- **What Happened?**: Despite the massive fundraising, the DAO lost the auction to another bidder. However, it showcased the speed and scale at which token-based communities can organize around a shared goal.

- **DAOs in Action**: Each contributor received $PEOPLE tokens as a representation of their participation. They intended to use these tokens to vote on certain governance aspects, such as what to do with the Constitution if they had won.

- **Takeaway**: Even though it didn't succeed in buying the document, ConstitutionDAO proved that strangers can quickly unite online, pool resources, and aim for a significant, real-world objective. It was a powerful demonstration of the potential of community tokens and DAOs.

3. Personal Tokens by Creators

Multiple artists and influencers have launched personal tokens to deepen fan engagement:

- **Examples**: RAC (a Grammy-winning musician) launched a social token called $RAC, giving fans perks like exclusive content and access to a community Discord.

- **Why It Matters**: This model flips the

typical relationship where artists rely on platforms (record labels, streaming services) for income. Instead, they can directly reward and engage their most supportive fans. Fans, in turn, can see the value of their tokens grow if the artist's popularity increases.

4. Gitcoin and Open-Source Communities

Open-source software often struggles with funding. **Gitcoin** is a platform that uses token-based incentives to reward developers for building and maintaining open-source projects. Contributors earn tokens for completing tasks or achieving milestones, aligning everyone's incentives toward improving shared software.

- **DAO Governance**: Gitcoin also has a DAO that decides how to allocate funds. Token holders can vote on which projects or grants deserve support.

- **Impact**: This approach has directed millions of dollars to open-source efforts, proving that token-based communities can solve age-old coordination problems outside of purely financial or social spheres.

5. Brand Loyalty Tokens

Some companies have experimented with **brand tokens** to replace or augment traditional loyalty points. Instead of airline miles or coffee punch cards, you'd hold a branded token that might unlock discounts or freebies.

- **Pros**: The tokens can be traded, potentially giving them real value on the market, and loyalty becomes more transparent (no hidden points system).

- **Cons**: Regulatory and user adoption hurdles are still high. But as user-friendly wallets emerge, brand tokens might become more common.

6. Local Community Tokens

Certain towns or neighborhoods are testing local

tokens that incentivize residents to shop at local businesses or volunteer at community events. Holding these tokens might grant discounts at local stores or pay for public services.

- **Aim**: Strengthen community ties by rewarding behaviors that benefit everyone, like attending council meetings or picking up litter.

- **Challenges**: Low digital literacy can hamper adoption, and the token's utility might be limited if not enough local businesses accept it. Still, the concept shows how tokens can foster real-world neighborly cooperation.

Lessons from These Examples

1. **Speed and Scale**: Token-based communities can form quickly, gather resources, and make a large impact in a short time.

2. **Incentive Alignment**: When everyone has a stake, they're more likely to contribute actively.

3. **Cultural Shift**: These examples go beyond tech-savvy corners—artists, local communities, and nonprofits are exploring tokens as well.

4. **Risk and Reward**: Speculative mania can overshadow the real utility, so communities must remain focused on their core missions.

5. **Experimentation Continues**: We're still early in seeing how tokens intersect with everyday life, but the building blocks are in place for innovative new models of collaboration and governance.

Bringing It All Together

Token-based communities represent an emerging paradigm in online (and offline) group organization, bridging technology, economics, and social dynamics. Here's a concise summary of what we've covered:

1. **Tokens Are More Than Money**

   - They can be membership passes, governance tools, loyalty points, or creative collectibles.

   - Fungible tokens serve as a shared stake; non-fungible tokens can be unique items or badges.

2. **Community and Social Tokens**

   - Groups use tokens to reward engagement, fund projects, and unify members around a shared vision.

   - Creators and influencers can issue social tokens that grant special perks to their audience.

3. **DAOs**

- Decentralized Autonomous Organizations employ tokens to let members vote on proposals and manage a communal treasury.

- They can range from investment clubs and social gatherings to open-source project funding or real-world asset acquisitions.

4. **Real-World Examples**

- **Friends with Benefits**: A social DAO turned cultural membership club.

- **ConstitutionDAO**: A short-lived but highly successful crowdfunding effort that highlighted collective power.

- **Gitcoin**: Supporting open-source development through token-based rewards.

- Local community tokens: Encouraging hometown involvement and shopping at local businesses.

Why It Matters for Non-Technical Audiences

You might wonder, "I'm not a developer or a crypto geek—why should I care?" Token-based communities matter because they represent a new way to:

- **Foster Belonging**: People can rally around a cause or interest in a more direct, meaningful way—owning a piece of the project rather than just observing it.

- **Encourage Creativity and Collaboration**: Tokens enable micro-incentives that reward people for specific contributions (e.g., writing an article, creating artwork, or hosting an event).

- **Redefine Economics and Governance**:

By distributing ownership and decision-making, communities can become more resilient, transparent, and inclusive, challenging the "top-down" norm.

- **Build Direct Relationships**: Whether you're an artist connecting with fans or a company building loyalty, tokens let you engage without relying exclusively on big middleman platforms.

Potential Pitfalls and Critiques

- **Speculation**: Some might buy community tokens purely to flip them for profit, leading to wild price swings and drama.

- **Complexity**: Setting up wallets, understanding private keys, and dealing with blockchain transactions can be confusing for newcomers. User-friendly solutions are improving but still evolving.

- **Regulation**: Laws surrounding token

offerings and securities vary by country. Groups must tread carefully to avoid legal issues.

- **Security Risks**: If a token contract or DAO system is hacked or poorly designed, members can lose funds or data.

- **Participation Overload**: In a DAO, having every small decision go to a community vote can lead to "voter fatigue" or bureaucracy. It's a balancing act between decentralization and practicality.

Looking Forward

Over the coming years, expect to see:

1. **More Mainstream Platforms**: Simplified tools that let non-technical users create or join token-based communities without fuss.

2. **Token Integration with Familiar Apps**: Social media, messaging platforms, and

online games might begin incorporating token-based rewards or memberships seamlessly.

3. **Expansion of Use Cases**: From local governance (city or county-level tokens) to philanthropic efforts (charities distributing tokens to donors), the possibilities are vast.

4. **Cultural Shift in Ownership**: As more people experience the power of co-ownership and co-governance, centralized platforms may feel outdated or exploitative by comparison.

In many ways, token-based communities echo the earliest days of the internet—optimistic, experimental, and brimming with potential. Just as Web1 introduced us to websites and email, and Web2 gave us social media and user-generated content, **Web3** (powered by tokens, decentralized tech, and new governance models) could redefine how we gather, share resources, and solve problems together.

Final Thoughts

Token-based communities offer a glimpse into a future where you're not just a spectator or a customer—you're also a stakeholder. Whether it's a local group launching a neighborhood improvement token, an artist sharing partial ownership of their creative output, or a global DAO solving environmental issues, the common thread is **collaboration fueled by aligned incentives**.

For non-technical folks, the underlying details (like how to deploy a smart contract) matter less than the broader benefits: autonomy, transparency, and a sense of genuine community ownership. If you've ever felt frustrated by corporate-controlled platforms or top-down organizations, token-based communities provide an alternative that's engaging, inclusive, and adaptive.

No doubt, challenges lie ahead—technical, legal, cultural. But the **core idea** is here to stay: People gather around shared tokens that represent membership, governance, or simply passion. And in doing so, they build something bigger than themselves, forging bonds that transcend borders and backgrounds.

The key takeaway is that tokens are **not just about money**. They're about **people** and the relationships they choose to nurture. They're about forging digital communities that can have real-world impact, from artistic collaborations to political activism. They're about enabling new ways to support creators, entrepreneurs, and innovators. Ultimately, they're about putting power back into the hands of the very people who make any community thrive—its members.

So whether you're a casual observer or someone eager to jump in, keep your eye on token-based communities. They represent one of the most dynamic frontiers in Web3, pushing us all to reconsider how we organize, cooperate, and share in the value we create together.

Chapter Highlights

1. **Tokens Are Multifaceted**: They can denote membership, social prestige, voting rights, and more, beyond mere monetary value.

2. **Social Tokens**: Creators and communities use them to foster tighter bonds with fans or members, rewarding engagement in new ways.

3. **DAOs**: The organizational backbone for many token-based communities, emphasizing shared governance and transparency.

4. **Real-World Applications**: From artistic endeavors (RAC, FWB) to philanthropic efforts (ConstitutionDAO), tokens have

shown they can rally large groups swiftly.

5. **Potential and Caution**: While the promise is big—democratizing ownership and decision-making—risks like speculation, complexity, and regulatory concerns remain.

Up Next: As our exploration of Web3 continues, keep in mind how token-based communities could intersect with **user-owned data**, **decentralized identity**, and **new economic models**. Each chapter in this book builds on the last, painting a picture of a future internet that's increasingly shaped by the people who use it, rather than a small elite of corporate gatekeepers.

If you find the concept inspiring, you might explore joining an existing token-based community, even if only to lurk and learn. Or you could consider launching your own token-based project if you have a cause or passion that resonates with a broader audience. Either way, remember that at the heart of every token-based community is the principle of

shared ownership—and that idea has the potential to reshape how we interact, create, and thrive in the digital age.

Chapter 6: User-Owned Data and Privacy

We live in a world where our digital lives are often spread across countless platforms—social media sites, online stores, apps on our phones—each collecting, analyzing, and sometimes selling information about our activities. Whether you're posting pictures of your family vacation or browsing for a new pair of shoes, your data is typically hoarded by centralized companies that profit from it. In this environment, phrases like "big data" and "data mining" can feel abstract yet ominous, hinting that we have lost control over who sees what about us online.

Web3 proposes an alternative: an internet in which **you**, the user, **own your data**. It envisions a future where you decide how and when to share personal information, and you can even potentially profit from it if you choose to. This new approach leans on decentralization, cryptography, and community governance to break away from the data silos controlled by tech giants. Yet, it also presents new challenges—self-management, privacy responsibilities, potential legal gray areas, and more.

This chapter explores what user-owned data means in the Web3 context, how privacy and security can be enhanced, and what practical tools are available today to help you start taking control of your digital life. By the end, you should have a clearer sense of how Web3 can bring about greater autonomy over personal data—without needing a Ph.D. in computer science or cryptography.

We'll tackle the following sections:

1. **How Data Ownership Works in Web3**

2. **Privacy & Security Advantages**

3. **Risks, Limitations, and Responsibilities**

4. **Everyday Tools and Apps for Data**

6.1 How Data Ownership Works in Web3

The Status Quo: Centralized Data Hoarding

In **Web2**—the internet most of us know—you typically sign up for platforms by handing over personal details. You create a username, give an email address, sometimes a phone number, and agree to lengthy terms of service that let the company store, analyze, and often monetize your data. Whether you're posting statuses on social media or buying groceries online, the platform gets to keep a record of your activities. It decides (within the boundaries of law and its own policies) how to use this information—targeted ads, personalized content recommendations, or, in some cases, selling data insights to third parties.

You effectively lose significant control the moment you click "I agree." While you can request data deletion in some regions thanks to laws like the General Data Protection Regulation (GDPR) in the European Union, the process is often cumbersome, and there's no absolute guarantee your data is truly erased from every backup or server.

The Web3 Breakthrough: Self-Sovereign Data

Web3 flips this dynamic. Rather than storing your data on a company's private servers, the idea is for **you** to keep it in a decentralized way—often in **wallets** or in **distributed storage systems** that only you can unlock. We sometimes call this concept **"self-sovereign data"** because you're the sovereign (the ultimate authority) over your digital identity and content.

Here's a simplified way to understand it:

- **Digital Wallets**: These are apps (or hardware devices) that store your **private keys**—unique cryptographic codes that grant access to your crypto assets, NFTs, and increasingly, your personal information or credentials. Instead of Facebook storing your photos, for instance, you might keep them encrypted in your own data vault or on a decentralized network, and use your private key to grant or deny access to others.

- **Decentralized Storage**: Systems like IPFS (InterPlanetary File System) or Arweave break your files into pieces and distribute them across many computers (nodes). Each piece is typically encrypted. When you or someone you authorize wants to retrieve the data, the network reassembles it, but only with the correct access permissions.

- **Smart Contracts and Verifiable Credentials**: If you need to prove something about yourself—such as your age, qualification, or membership in a community—you share a digitally signed credential rather than handing over raw personal data. This can drastically reduce the amount of sensitive info you're forced to disclose to apps or websites.

Ownership vs. Permission

Data ownership in Web3 often boils down to **control**. In the old model, you gave up control by uploading your files or credentials to a company's server. In Web3, your data might live in a decentralized space, but you alone hold the cryptographic keys that grant access. You decide who can see it, for how long, and under what conditions.

For instance, suppose an online store wants your shipping address. Rather than storing your address in their database permanently, you might share it with them in an **encrypted transaction** that's only valid for one delivery. Once the transaction is completed, they can't keep accessing your address unless you authorize it again. This is a stark contrast to typical e-commerce sites that keep your address on file indefinitely.

Incentives and Tokenization

One unique twist in the Web3 realm is the potential for **tokenizing** data or rewarding users for sharing their data. Instead of a platform profiting solely from your activity, you might receive tokens or other benefits whenever you allow your data to be used. This could be as small as getting micro-rewards for consenting to data analytics or as large as receiving governance tokens in a community that uses your data for research or product development.

Of course, this isn't to say you **have** to profit from your data—some people will prefer strict privacy. But Web3 tools give you the **option** to treat your data as an asset you can lend, trade, or withhold, shifting power away from centralized corporations that currently enjoy a near-monopoly on data-driven profits.

A Gradual Transition

The technology for full self-sovereign data is still maturing. Many apps are "hybrid," storing some information on centralized servers (for speed or convenience) and some on decentralized networks. Giant platforms like YouTube or Instagram haven't gone Web3-native, so if you want to share your videos or photos widely, you might still rely on traditional sites. But the **direction** is clear: as more user-friendly decentralized apps (dApps) emerge, controlling your data will become easier, more intuitive, and more widely adopted.

The key takeaway is that **data ownership in Web3** isn't just about "blocking ads" or "hiding your profile." It's about a fundamental reorientation: **you** become the gatekeeper, deciding who gets to see, use, or benefit from your personal information. That shift underpins the privacy and security advantages we'll discuss next.

6.2 Privacy & Security Advantages

Privacy by Design

In Web2, privacy often feels like an afterthought. Companies build platforms to collect as much information as possible—then they patch in privacy features or disclaimers later, usually under legal or public pressure. In contrast, **Web3** emphasizes "privacy by design." Because so many Web3 systems revolve around cryptography and user-owned data vaults, privacy isn't just a setting you toggle on; it's baked into the architecture.

- **No Single Point of Failure**: With user-owned data, there's no giant central server housing everything. If one node in the decentralized network is compromised, it doesn't automatically expose all data. This makes mass data breaches less likely.

- **Encrypted by Default**: Many decentralized apps encourage or even require encryption at every step. This means that even if data is intercepted, it's indecipherable without the right keys.

- **Selective Disclosure**: Instead of handing over your entire profile (like name, address, phone number), you can reveal only the minimal facts necessary for a transaction. Imagine proving you're over 18 without sharing your birthday—**zero-knowledge proofs** and other cryptographic techniques enable precisely that kind of privacy-preserving interaction.

Defending Against Surveillance

Web3 also holds promise as an antidote to widespread surveillance—whether by corporations, governments, or malicious hackers. In many decentralized applications, you interact via wallet addresses or pseudonymous digital identities, rather than your real name or email. This can make tracking your movements online more difficult.

- **Pseudonymity vs. Anonymity**: While pseudonymity isn't the same as total anonymity, it's often enough to protect casual users from targeted data harvesting. If you choose, you can have multiple wallet addresses: one for your NFT gaming, another for interacting with social dApps, another for professional credentials— keeping these aspects of your online life separate.

- **Censorship Resistance**: In some contexts, certain centralized platforms block or throttle content based on location or political concerns. A decentralized, user-owned data system can be harder to censor. Files stored on IPFS or Arweave, for example, remain accessible as long as nodes keep hosting them. No single company can just "take them down."

Security at a Personal and Systemic Level

Decentralization can enhance **personal security** as well as the **overall resilience** of the network:

- **Personal Security**: Owning your data means you're not relying on a platform's security measures to protect your passwords or private information. Yes, it places more responsibility on you (we'll discuss that soon), but it also reduces the risk that a breach on a social network's database will leak your personal details.

- **Network Resilience**: With no single point of failure, decentralized systems can continue to run even if parts of the network go offline. This makes them appealing for critical services that can't afford downtime or catastrophic data losses.

The Trade-Offs

All this isn't to claim Web3 is a privacy utopia. Blockchain transactions are **inherently transparent** in many cases: if you use a public blockchain like Ethereum, your wallet address and transaction history are visible to anyone who knows how to look it up. That's why privacy-oriented technologies (such as **Zero-Knowledge Proofs**, **privacy coins**, or **layer-2 networks** with encryption) are so crucial. They aim to blend the benefits of decentralization with confidentiality.

But as a baseline, the shift from "company holds your data" to "you hold your data and reveal it selectively" is a monumental step toward stronger privacy. It's akin to living in your own locked house rather than constantly crashing on someone else's couch where they can rummage through your stuff at will.

6.3 Risks, Limitations, and Responsibilities

The "Self-Custody" Challenge

When people talk about user-owned data, a big theme is **"self-custody."** In the crypto world, self-custody means you hold your private keys. No bank or platform can freeze your funds if they get hacked, nor can they seize your assets due to arbitrary policy changes. The same principle applies to data: you hold the keys that grant access to your information.

While this is empowering, it also means you bear the burden of **responsibility**. If you lose your private keys or forget your seed phrase, you might be locked out of your own data forever. There's no "forgot password" button in a fully decentralized system. This can be a scary prospect for people used to calling up customer service whenever they lose access.

Complexity and Usability Gaps

Another limitation is **usability**. Web3 tools often lag behind Web2 platforms in terms of polished interfaces and smooth experiences. Setting up a wallet, learning about seed phrases, using decentralized storage, or dealing with complicated transaction fees can be intimidating. Non-technical users might struggle unless the tools are designed to be straightforward.

The community is working on solutions like:

- **Social Recovery**: Splitting your recovery phrase among trusted friends or family members, so no single person can hijack your account, but multiple people can help you recover it if you lose access.

- **Key Management Services**: Emerging platforms that offer user-friendly ways to handle cryptographic keys, potentially storing encrypted backups across multiple locations.

- **Layer-2 Scalability**: Systems that cut down on fees and speed up transactions so that Web3 apps can be as quick as Web2 apps.

Regulatory and Legal Ambiguities

If you store data in a decentralized network that spans multiple countries, whose laws apply if there's a dispute? How do regulations like the

GDPR's "right to be forgotten" work in a system where data might be spread across hundreds of nodes? These legal questions are complex and still evolving.

- **Personal Liability**: If you store certain types of data (e.g., copyrighted material or sensitive info) in a public, decentralized manner, are you liable if it's leaked or misused?

- **Tax and Financial Implications**: If you earn tokens or money by sharing data, that may have taxation consequences in your jurisdiction.

Most experts believe legal frameworks will adapt over time, but for now, early adopters of Web3 technology face some regulatory uncertainty. It's wise to stay informed about relevant policies in your region.

Transparency vs. Privacy

As noted, many blockchains are public by default. While your address might be pseudonymous, an adept analyst could potentially link your on-chain activity to your real identity, especially if you've interacted with centralized crypto exchanges or used personal data somewhere in the chain.

This tension between transparency and privacy is a double-edged sword. On the one hand, the open ledger fosters trust: you can verify that transactions really took place, that funds weren't misused, etc. On the other hand, it can be a privacy nightmare if your every move can be traced.

Potential for Exploitation and Scams

Web3, like any emerging field, attracts scammers. Fraudulent sites may pretend to be genuine decentralized apps, encouraging you to link your wallet—and thereby draining your funds or stealing your data. Phishing attacks, rug pulls, and malicious smart contracts are real threats.

Vigilance is essential. Because no centralized

authority can simply undo a malicious transaction, once you sign a transaction granting a scammer access to your tokens or data, it might be gone for good. Tools that provide transaction simulation, reputation checks for smart contracts, and community auditing can help mitigate these risks.

Balancing Accessibility with Responsibility

In short, user-owned data in Web3 is a **paradigm shift**—but it's not a silver bullet or a carefree ride. You gain autonomy, privacy, and control, but you also shoulder new responsibilities. If you prefer a fully managed service with a support hotline, you might have to wait until user-friendly, partially decentralized solutions become mainstream. Alternatively, you can start experimenting with user-owned data tools now, but proceed carefully, learn best practices, and accept the learning curve that comes with genuine digital sovereignty.

6.4 Everyday Tools and Apps for Data

Ownership

Now that we've explored the whys and hows of user-owned data, let's dive into **practical** solutions available today. While we're still in the early stages, a growing number of tools and apps aim to make decentralized data management more accessible and intuitive.

1. Decentralized Storage Solutions

1. **IPFS (InterPlanetary File System)**

   o **What It Is**: A peer-to-peer file sharing system that uses content-based addressing instead of traditional URLs. This means files are found by their cryptographic "fingerprint" (hash), and can be served by multiple nodes.

   o **Why It Matters**: You can upload files (like documents, images, or even websites) to IPFS, and they remain retrievable as long as at least one node (including you) hosts them. No single entity can arbitrarily remove them.

- ○ **Use Case**: Storing personal documents or website assets in a censorship-resistant manner.

2. **Arweave**

- ○ **What It Is**: A "permanent" storage network using a technology called blockweave. It's designed for data permanence, incentivizing participants to store files indefinitely.

- ○ **Why It Matters**: Once you pay to store something on Arweave, it's intended to stay there forever. This can be ideal for archiving important historical data, documents, or creative works you never want lost.

- Use Case: Archiving family photos, research data, or public records in a tamper-proof environment.

3. **Filecoin**

   - **What It Is**: A decentralized storage marketplace built on top of IPFS, where users can rent out spare hard drive space and get paid in Filecoin tokens.

   - **Why It Matters**: It creates a marketplace for data storage, potentially lowering costs and increasing redundancy.

   - **Use Case**: Storing larger datasets in a distributed manner, with a marketplace-based approach to pricing and capacity.

For non-technical users, these platforms might feel unfamiliar at first, but user-friendly interfaces are gradually emerging. Some Web3 projects bundle IPFS or Arweave under the hood, meaning you might not even realize you're using a decentralized storage network.

2. Self-Sovereign Identity (SSI) Wallets

1. **Metamask, Rainbow, or Other Crypto Wallets**

   o **What They Are**: Wallets primarily used for holding cryptocurrencies and NFTs. While they don't all natively store personal data like passports or health records, they're an entry point into Web3.

   o **Why They Matter**: These wallets teach you how to manage private keys and interact with decentralized apps (dApps). Some expansions or plugins can store additional credentials.

2. **Dedicated SSI Wallets**

o **Example**: Solutions like **uPort** (one of the early movers, though it has changed over time), **Evernym** or **Trinsic** in the SSI space. They focus on storing verifiable credentials— digital proofs that might confirm your age, qualifications, or membership in an organization—on your device.

o **Why They Matter**: If you want to truly own your identity data (like a driver's license, professional certifications, or even loyalty memberships), these wallets let you hold them personally, not on a central server.

3. **Social Recovery and Multi-Sig**

o **What It Is**: Some wallets support a feature where multiple trusted friends (or devices) can collectively help you recover access if you lose your main key. In "multi-sig" (multi-signature) setups, major actions require multiple approvals.

- o **Why It Matters**: Reduces the risk of losing everything if you misplace your seed phrase or your hardware wallet. It's a user-friendly step toward safer self-custody.

3. Private Communications Tools

1. **Encrypted Messaging Apps**

   - o **Examples**: Signal, Session, or Matrix. While not all are purely Web3, they emphasize end-to-end encryption and minimal data collection.

   - o **Why They Matter**: Communication is part of our daily digital footprint. Using apps that store minimal metadata and rely on user-owned encryption keys can reduce data leaks or government/corporate snooping.

2. **Decentralized Social Networks**

   o **Examples**: Lens Protocol, Mastodon (federated, though not fully on blockchain), or Minds.

   o **Why They Matter**: Instead of giving control over your content to Twitter or Facebook, you post on networks where you or a community server retains ownership. Some projects let you store posts on IPFS or a similar decentralized layer, so your data can't be easily deleted or monetized without your consent.

3. **Email Alternatives**

   o **Examples**: ProtonMail (end-to-end encryption), Skiff (Web3-inspired email and file sharing).

- o **Why They Matter**: Email remains a big data leak vector, as many free email providers scan messages for ad targeting. Secure email with user-owned encryption keys cuts out that snooping.

4. Privacy-Focused Browsers and Search Engines

1. **Brave Browser**

   - o **What It Is**: A Chromium-based browser that blocks ads and trackers by default, and allows opt-in ads that reward you in Basic Attention Token (BAT).

   - o **Why It Matters**: Instead of having your data quietly tracked, you choose if you want to see ads—and you get a share of the revenue. It's a step toward user-owned browsing data.

2. **Presearch**

   o **What It Is**: A decentralized search engine that rewards users in PRE tokens for searching.

   o **Why It Matters**: It attempts to avoid the data-collection arms race typical of major search engines, giving users control over how they engage with searches and advertisements.

5. Data Marketplaces and Monetization

1. **Ocean Protocol**

   o **What It Is**: A blockchain-based marketplace where individuals (or companies) can sell access to datasets while still keeping them private. Buyers can run computations on the data without directly seeing it.

   o **Why It Matters**: If you want to

monetize, say, your health or fitness data for medical research, you can do so in a controlled manner. This flips the script on data brokers who collect and sell data without rewarding the original owners.

2. **Reputation and Lending Platforms**

- **What They Are**: Some DeFi (decentralized finance) platforms let you use data-driven reputation to get better lending rates or opportunities. Rather than a traditional credit score from a central agency, you present on-chain proof of financial reliability.

- **Why They Matter**: You own the underlying data or transaction history, and you reveal only what's necessary for a loan. You might keep your identity pseudonymous but still prove a track record of repayment.

6. Everyday Best Practices

Even if you're not ready to fully dive into these tools, a few daily habits can help ease you into a user-owned data mindset:

- **Use Strong, Unique Passwords**: Or better yet, passphrases. A password manager (though not necessarily Web3) is an excellent starting point for personal security.

- **Enable Two-Factor Authentication (2FA)**: Wherever possible. This reduces the risk of account takeovers.

- **Be Wary of Phishing**: Double-check URLs, especially when connecting a crypto wallet to a new site. Bookmark official websites and never click on random links in unsolicited messages.

- **Back Up Your Seed Phrases**: If you use a Web3 wallet, keep multiple secure backups (written down or stored on an encrypted drive in different physical locations).

- **Stay Informed**: Follow reputable sources that track developments in decentralized tech. The landscape changes quickly, and new user-friendly tools appear all the time.

A Glimpse Ahead

As the Web3 ecosystem continues to evolve, we can expect more seamless integrations. We might see social media platforms that let you post your content on IPFS by default, or streaming services that encrypt your watch history so only you control who knows your viewing habits. Meanwhile, self-sovereign identity solutions could replace the "login with Facebook" model, letting you retain full ownership of your profile data across multiple sites.

For now, if you're intrigued by the idea of truly owning your data, the best approach is to

experiment with small steps. Perhaps try out a privacy-focused browser, explore a decentralized social platform, or store a few files on IPFS. These incremental experiences will help you get comfortable with the Web3 mindset and prepare you for a future where user-owned data might be the norm rather than the exception.

Conclusion

User-owned data represents one of the most fundamental shifts in the Web3 vision. Instead of living at the mercy of big tech's data collection and monetization engines, you become the **custodian** of your digital footprint. Privacy, once considered a luxury or afterthought, becomes a built-in feature. This transition isn't without its complications—self-custody can be daunting, and regulations still lag behind the technology. But the gains in autonomy, security, and empowerment are immense.

Let's recap the key points:

1. **How Data Ownership Works in Web3**: Shifting from centralized servers to decentralized networks, you control your files, credentials, and personal details via cryptographic keys.

2. **Privacy & Security Advantages**: By design, Web3 can minimize big data breaches and corporate surveillance, offering selective disclosure and encryption as standard features.

3. **Risks, Limitations, and Responsibilities**: Self-custody means you're in charge of your keys; lose them, and you might lose access permanently. Usability gaps, legal gray areas, and on-chain transparency also pose challenges.

4. **Everyday Tools and Apps for Data Ownership**: A range of decentralized storage platforms, identity wallets, privacy-focused browsers, and data marketplaces are

pioneering the user-owned approach, although these tools are still evolving.

For non-technical audiences, the prospect of setting up wallets, securing seed phrases, or using decentralized storage may sound complex. But remember: much like the early days of the internet, user-friendly interfaces and step-by-step guides will keep improving. Early adopters—be they curious individuals, community groups, or small businesses—can help shape the usability of these solutions by providing feedback, forming local "Web3 meetups," or simply sharing experiences online.

Ultimately, user-owned data is about **freedom and choice**. It's the freedom to decide who sees your information and under what conditions. It's the choice to break away from privacy-invading norms and create a digital life where your consent truly matters. In a world growing more dependent on data by the minute, reclaiming that autonomy might just be the key to a healthier, more respectful, and more equitable internet.

Chapter Highlights

- **User-owned data** counters the centralized data hoarding of Web2. Rather than multiple corporations holding your personal info, **you** keep it under your own cryptographic keys.

- **Privacy by design** in Web3 means no single point of failure, stronger encryption, and the ability to share only minimal necessary information.

- **Self-custody** can be both empowering and risky; lose your private keys, and you lose your data. This introduces a new level of personal responsibility.

- Despite current **usability hurdles** and regulatory uncertainties, everyday tools (like IPFS, Arweave, decentralized identity wallets, or privacy browsers) already exist to help you explore user-owned data today.

- The long-term vision is a more equitable, secure, and privacy-respecting digital world—if we embrace the ethos and tools of **decentralization**.

As you move forward in this book, remember that data ownership connects closely with other Web3 pillars, such as decentralized identity, token-based communities, and smart contracts. A truly user-centered internet depends on each of these elements reinforcing the others—giving you more control, more choices, and ultimately, a stronger voice in shaping the digital ecosystems you inhabit.

Chapter 7: Navigating Web3: Practical Tips and Tools

For many newcomers, **Web3** can seem daunting—wallets, private keys, tokens, blockchains, and a whole new world of decentralized applications. Yet, in many ways, stepping into this new internet paradigm is reminiscent of going online for the first time in the 1990s: you're learning a fresh set of tools, acronyms, and cultural norms. The good news is that once you grasp the fundamentals, you'll discover a wide array of opportunities: online communities that reward your participation, financial services free from traditional gatekeepers, and new ways to express and share your digital identity.

This chapter is meant to function as your **practical roadmap**. It's not going to transform you into an overnight crypto expert, but it will help you **avoid common pitfalls** and start your journey with more confidence. Think of it like a traveler's guide to a foreign country: you'll learn how to get your passport (the wallet), navigate the local customs (dApps and marketplaces), make friends and join local clubs (DAOs), and keep a checklist so you don't lose track of important details.

By the time you finish reading, you'll have a clearer idea of how to set up a wallet securely, what to look for in the dApp ecosystem, how to join or even start a DAO, and which beginner tasks will help you practice these skills step by step.

7.1 Getting a Wallet and Securing It

7.1.1 Why You Need a Wallet in Web3

In **Web2**, you might log into a website using an email and password, or even log in with Google or Facebook credentials. In **Web3**, however, your entry point is typically a **crypto wallet**. This wallet doesn't just store digital currencies; it also manages your access to decentralized apps and networks.

You can think of it as both your personal bank account and your online "passport," containing the cryptographic keys that prove you own whatever digital assets (tokens, NFTs, or other forms of digital identity) are associated with your address.

A Web3 wallet is crucial because it:

1. **Manages Your Private Keys**: These keys confirm your identity on a blockchain network. If you own tokens or NFTs, you can only access them by proving you hold the correct private key.

2. **Facilitates Transactions**: If you want to swap tokens, buy an NFT, or vote in a decentralized autonomous organization (DAO), your wallet signs the transaction.

3. **Stores Credentials**: Beyond just currency, wallets can hold proof of membership (like DAO tokens) or even data about your identity (such as verifiable credentials).

7.1.2 Types of Wallets

When you're just starting out, you'll likely encounter two major types of wallets:

1. **Software Wallets** (Hot Wallets)

    o **Examples**: MetaMask, Trust Wallet, Rainbow, Phantom (for Solana), etc.

    o **How They Work**: These wallets are apps or browser extensions that keep your private keys on your phone or computer. They're called "hot" because they're connected to the internet whenever your device is online.

    o **Pros**: Easy to set up, user-friendly, quick for daily transactions.

    o **Cons**: If your device gets hacked or infected with malware, your private keys could be compromised.

2. **Hardware Wallets** (Cold Wallets)

o **Examples**: Ledger, Trezor, Keystone.

o **How They Work**: These are physical devices (like a USB stick) that keep your private keys offline most of the time. When you want to make a transaction, you connect the wallet to your computer or phone and approve the transaction on the device.

o **Pros**: Far more secure against online threats, as keys are stored in a sealed environment.

o **Cons**: They're not free (devices can cost $50–$200) and slightly less convenient for everyday use.

There are also **paper wallets** (literally printing your keys on paper) and **smart contract wallets** (which add extra features like multi-signature), but for most beginners, a software wallet is the fastest way to start experimenting with Web3. Once you hold a bit more value in your wallet or become more serious about security, you might invest in a hardware wallet.

7.1.3 Securing Your Wallet

Security is paramount in Web3 because there's no "password reset" service if something goes wrong. You're responsible for safeguarding your assets. Here are some tips to ensure you don't lose control:

1. **Seed Phrase Backup**: When you first set up a wallet, it generates a **seed phrase** (usually 12–24 words). Write these words down on paper (not in a digital document or cloud storage) and keep multiple copies in safe places. If you lose this phrase or someone else obtains it, your assets could be lost or stolen.

2. **Use Strong Passwords**: Most software

wallets let you set an additional password or PIN. Don't reuse one from another account—pick something unique and secure.

3. **Enable Two-Factor Authentication (2FA)**: If the wallet or service allows it, 2FA adds another layer of protection.

4. **Beware of Phishing**: Scammers often create fake websites resembling popular wallet apps or dApps. Always double-check the URL before you connect your wallet.

5. **Consider a Hardware Wallet**: If you start holding tokens or NFTs of significant value, a hardware wallet is worth the investment. It adds a physical barrier to hacking attempts.

7.1.4 Testing and Practice

Before diving in with large amounts of money or vital assets, do a **test run**. Transfer a small amount of crypto from an exchange to your new wallet. Try sending some tokens to a friend or to another address you control. The small fees paid for these transactions can be viewed as "practice fees," ensuring you understand the process before bigger stakes are on the line.

Remember, **start small**, keep your seed phrase safe, and never share it with anyone (no legitimate site or service will ask for it). With a well-secured wallet, you've taken the first major step into Web3.

7.2 Exploring dApps and Marketplaces

7.2.1 What Are dApps?

A **decentralized application (dApp)** is a software program that runs on a blockchain or peer-to-peer network, rather than a single centralized server. Think of it as an application that can't be arbitrarily shut down or censored by a single authority. These dApps range from games and social media platforms to financial tools and marketplaces.

For the non-technical reader, the biggest difference you'll notice with a dApp is how you **log in** and **interact**. Instead of creating a username/password on the site's servers, you typically click a button labeled "Connect Wallet." Once your wallet is connected, the dApp recognizes your blockchain address. Anything you do—like swapping tokens, casting a vote, or posting content—will typically cost a small network fee (gas) and is recorded on the blockchain.

7.2.2 Types of dApps

1. **Decentralized Finance (DeFi)**

    o **Examples**: Uniswap, Aave, Compound.

    o **Use Case**: Borrow, lend, or swap tokens without a bank or broker. Earn interest on your crypto or take out a loan by providing collateral.

o **Risks**: Some protocols can be complex. Smart contract bugs or market volatility can lead to losses, so always research thoroughly before depositing large sums.

2. **NFT Marketplaces**

   o **Examples**: OpenSea, Rarible, Magic Eden (Solana).

   o **Use Case**: Buy, sell, and trade digital collectibles or artwork as NFTs (non-fungible tokens).

   o **Risks**: The NFT market can be highly speculative. Scams and counterfeits exist, and the value of collectibles is often subjective.

3. **Gaming dApps**

   o **Examples**: Axie Infinity, The Sandbox, Decentraland.

- Use Case: Play games to earn tokens or own in-game items as NFTs. Some games let you buy and sell virtual land or characters that you truly own in your wallet.

- Risks: Game economies can fluctuate. Some "play-to-earn" models rely on continued user growth, and if hype dies down, token prices can drop drastically.

4. **Social dApps**

- **Examples**: Lens Protocol, Minds, Mastodon (partially decentralized).

- **Use Case**: Social media platforms where users retain ownership of their content or profiles, and no single corporation can ban or deplatform them on a whim.

- **Risks**: Adoption can be smaller

compared to mainstream social platforms, so finding your community might take time.

5. **Tools and Utility dApps**

   o **Examples**: ENS (Ethereum Name Service) for human-readable wallet names, IPFS-based storage apps for decentralized file hosting.

   o **Use Case**: Replacing complicated addresses with easier ones (like "yourname.eth") or storing files in a way that's censorship-resistant.

   o **Risks**: Typically straightforward, but always confirm you're using legitimate versions of these tools, as scammers make copycat websites.

7.2.3 How to Interact with a dApp

- **Connect Your Wallet**: Most dApps have a "Connect Wallet" button. When you click it, your browser wallet (e.g., MetaMask) will pop up, asking if you want to grant the dApp permission to view your addresses or initiate transactions.

- **Approve Transactions**: If you want to perform an action—like swapping tokens or minting an NFT—you'll typically see a transaction request. Your wallet will detail the estimated gas fee, and you'll need to confirm or reject the transaction.

- **Check the Gas**: Depending on the blockchain, you may pay variable fees. Ethereum gas fees can be high during network congestion. Other chains (like Solana or Polygon) might be cheaper.

- **Record and Track**: Since everything is on-chain, you can view your transaction history on block explorers (e.g., Etherscan, Polygonscan) to confirm what happened and when.

7.2.4 Safety Tips for dApps

- **Use Trusted Links**: Bookmark official dApp websites or access them through reputable aggregator sites like Coingecko or CoinMarketCap.

- **Verify Smart Contract Addresses**: If you're buying a token or NFT, confirm you've got the correct contract address to avoid fakes.

- **Test with Small Amounts**: If you're unsure, do a small test transaction first.

- **Watch Out for Permissions**: Some dApps ask for permission to spend unlimited amounts of your tokens. Revoke those permissions when you're done if you're concerned about potential misuse (you can do this via "token approval" dashboards or your wallet's interface).

- **Stay Informed**: The Web3 landscape

changes quickly. Follow reliable news outlets, social media accounts, or community forums to keep up with security alerts and best practices.

Exploring dApps can be a fun, eye-opening experience, revealing the power of decentralized technology. By starting small, doing research, and using your wallet responsibly, you can unlock new ways to interact online—whether it's trading tokens, collecting digital art, or simply using a social network on your own terms.

7.3 Participating in a DAO

7.3.1 What Is a DAO Again?

You likely read about **DAOs (Decentralized Autonomous Organizations)** earlier in this book, but let's recap in plain language. A DAO is like an online community that uses tokens, smart contracts, and transparent voting to govern itself.

Instead of relying on a traditional hierarchy, decisions are made collectively: if you hold the community's governance token, you can propose or vote on new ideas.

To understand how this works, imagine a local club that holds a treasury of funds. Any member can propose how to spend the funds—maybe to buy supplies, plan an event, or invest in a collaborative project. Then all the members vote, and if the proposal passes, the money automatically moves from the club's shared account to the designated recipient. That's the gist of how a DAO treasury operates, except it happens on a blockchain, meaning no single person can override the collective's will.

7.3.2 Finding the Right DAO for You

DAOs exist for almost any interest or project:

1. **Investment DAOs**: Pool funds to invest in startups, NFTs, or other assets.

2. **Service/Work DAOs**: Gather talent (developers, designers, marketers) who collectively bid on projects and share profits.

3. **Social Clubs**: Focus on networking, art, music, or cultural events (like Friends with Benefits or Cabin DAO).

4. **Protocol DAOs**: Govern major DeFi platforms like Uniswap or MakerDAO.

5. **Media/Content DAOs**: Publish articles, curate media, and distribute revenue among contributors.

6. **Philanthropic DAOs**: Fundraise and distribute resources for social causes or nonprofit activities.

To find a DAO, you can browse aggregator sites (like DeepDAO, DAOhaus) or simply follow Web3 community channels (Twitter, Discord, Telegram). Look for a group whose mission, vibe, and values align with your own.

7.3.3 Joining a DAO

Each DAO has its own membership rules:

- **Token-Gated Entry**: Some DAOs require you to hold a certain number of governance tokens or an NFT that represents membership. Once in your wallet, you can join the DAO's private Discord or voting portal.

- **Open Membership**: A few DAOs let anyone participate in discussions, though you might need a token to actually vote.

- **Application Process**: Some specialized DAOs (like ones focusing on developer work) may ask you to apply or prove your skills before granting membership.

Once you're in, you'll often find channels or forums where proposals are discussed. You can contribute ideas, join sub-teams (like marketing, community building, or product development), and start shaping the organization.

7.3.4 How DAO Governance Works

- **Proposals**: Anyone with the requisite permission (e.g., a certain token balance or role) can draft a proposal, specifying what they want to do, why, and how much funding (if any) is needed.

- **Voting**: Proposals typically appear in a governance interface (often powered by a platform like Snapshot, Aragon, or Tally). DAO members connect their wallets to cast votes proportional to their token holdings or according to the DAO's rules.

- **Execution**: If a proposal passes, smart contracts automatically move funds or update settings. Some DAOs have a "multi-signature wallet" where multiple signers confirm the action, adding a layer of security.

- **Iterative Improvements**: DAOs often evolve—updating voting thresholds, changing how tokens are allocated, or even merging with other DAOs. Every significant change is subject to a vote.

7.3.5 Contributing Effectively

While DAO membership can be fun, it also requires initiative. Here's how to make the most of it:

1. **Learn the Culture**: Read old proposals, chat in the Discord, see what the DAO's ethos is.

2. **Start Small**: Volunteer for a small task— e.g., writing a newsletter, moderating a chat, or translating content. This helps you build credibility.

3. **Be Respectful**: DAOs can be global communities with diverse viewpoints. Constructive debate is encouraged; personal attacks are not.

4. **Offer Solutions**: Don't just point out problems; propose actionable fixes.

5. **Vote Thoughtfully**: Read proposals carefully, understand the implications, and consider the DAO's long-term goals.

7.3.6 Why Join a DAO?

DAOs are redefining how we collaborate online. They can foster a sense of **shared ownership**, encouraging more active participation than traditional social media groups. For many, DAOs also provide networking opportunities, skill-building experiences, and even financial rewards if the DAO's projects succeed. Whether you're a developer, artist, writer, marketer, or just curious, participating in a DAO can be a meaningful way to engage with Web3 beyond just trading tokens.

7.4 A Beginner's Checklist

You've learned about setting up a wallet, exploring

dApps, and joining DAOs. But if you're brand new, you might still wonder how to pull it all together. Here's a **step-by-step checklist** to help you navigate your early days in Web3:

7.4.1 Step 1: Do Some Basic Research

- **Read Reputable Guides**: Before you jump in, familiarize yourself with Web3 fundamentals. Stick to well-known resources or official documentation for the apps/wallets you'll use.

- **Watch Out for Hype**: Crypto and Web3 can be full of big promises. Keep your expectations realistic, and don't fall for "get rich quick" schemes.

Target Duration: A few hours or days, depending on your comfort level. Taking time here can save heartbreak later.

7.4.2 Step 2: Acquire a Small Amount of Crypto

- **Choose a Blockchain**: Ethereum is the most common for dApps, but it has higher fees. Cheaper options include Polygon, Solana, or Binance Smart Chain.

- **Buy Crypto on an Exchange**: If you're using Ethereum, buy some Ether (ETH) on a reputable exchange (Coinbase, Binance, Kraken, etc.). Transfer a small amount to your newly created wallet to cover transaction fees (gas).

- **Keep It Minimal**: Start with something like $50–$100 worth of crypto. Enough to experiment but not enough to cause major stress if things go wrong.

Target Duration: A few minutes to set up the exchange account (plus potential ID verification time), and a few minutes to transfer funds.

7.4.3 Step 3: Set Up and Secure Your Wallet

- **Choose a Wallet**: For beginners, a browser extension wallet like MetaMask (for Ethereum and related networks) is common. Alternatively, consider Trust Wallet or Rainbow.

- **Write Down Seed Phrase**: No screenshots, no typed notes—handwritten on paper, stored securely. Make multiple copies in different safe locations.

- **Add Network Settings**: If you plan to use non-Ethereum chains (like Polygon, Arbitrum, or BSC), you can manually add their network info in the wallet's settings or use a service like Chainlist.org.

- **Protect Your Wallet**: Set a strong password or PIN. If you can, enable biometric authentication on your phone (like fingerprint or Face ID).

Target Duration: 15–30 minutes to install and configure everything.

7.4.4 Step 4: Practice Basic Transactions

- **Send a Test Amount**: Transfer a few dollars of ETH (or another token) from your exchange to your wallet. Confirm it arrives.

- **Try a Token Swap**: On a platform like Uniswap or a simpler exchange aggregator (like 1inch or Matcha), swap a small amount of ETH for a stablecoin (USDC or DAI). Watch how gas fees and slippage behave.

- **Check a Block Explorer**: Visit Etherscan (for Ethereum) or Polygonscan (for Polygon) to see the transaction details. This helps you learn how on-chain data is recorded.

Target Duration: 15–45 minutes, factoring in any

delays or confirmations needed.

7.4.5 Step 5: Explore a Simple dApp or NFT Marketplace

- **Choose a User-Friendly dApp**: Maybe you're curious about NFT art. Head to OpenSea (for Ethereum-based NFTs) or a cheaper alternative on Polygon.

- **Connect Your Wallet**: A pop-up from MetaMask (or your chosen wallet) should appear. Approve the connection.

- **Browse or Test-Mint**: Look for free or low-cost NFTs if you want to experiment. Some projects do "free mints," letting you pay only the gas fee.

- **Don't Overspend**: Stick to small purchases to learn the ropes—NFT mania can be expensive if you chase the hype.

Target Duration: 30–60 minutes to browse, connect, mint, or buy something small.

7.4.6 Step 6: Join a DAO Community

- **Pick a DAO**: If you're into art, look for an art collective DAO. If you're into social experiences, maybe a well-known community DAO. If you like DeFi, join a protocol's DAO.

- **Acquire Membership Token**: If needed, buy or claim the DAO's token or NFT (be sure it's the legitimate one).

- **Introduce Yourself**: Head to the DAO's Discord, say hello, and read up on proposals or pinned resources.

- **Add Value**: Look for a small task or discussion to contribute to. Don't be shy about asking how you can help.

Target Duration: Ongoing—DAO participation is more of a habit than a one-time task.

7.4.7 Step 7: Maintain Security Hygiene

- **Stay Alert**: Phishing scams often appear as direct messages on Discord, Twitter, or Telegram. Admins in reputable servers rarely DM you first.

- **Review Approvals**: Periodically, use token approval sites or your wallet's interface to check which dApps can access your tokens. Revoke unnecessary permissions.

- **Update Your Tools**: Keep your wallet, browser extension, and antivirus software up to date.

- **Consider Hardware Wallet**: If you're now holding more than you'd be comfortable losing, upgrade to a Ledger or Trezor to store your private keys offline.

Target Duration: Ongoing—security is never a one-and-done deal.

7.4.8 Step 8: Scale Up or Dial Down

After you've spent a few weeks or months in Web3:

- **Reflect**: Does this align with your goals? Are you primarily interested in finance, art, gaming, or community building? Focus on the areas that bring you value and enjoyment.

- **Diversify Your Knowledge**: If you want to try new blockchains (Solana, Avalanche, Tezos, etc.), repeat the steps with small amounts of funds to learn their ecosystems.

- **Educate Others**: Helping friends and family set up wallets can be rewarding but do it carefully—teach them about security from the start so they don't learn the hard way.

- **Stay Curious**: Web3 is a fast-evolving field. Keep up with reputable news outlets, Twitter threads from experts, or join online meetups to expand your knowledge and adapt to changes.

Target Duration: However long you want. There's no rush; many enthusiasts spend years exploring all corners of Web3.

Putting It All Together

These steps outline a journey that might take you anywhere from a weekend to several months. The key is to **pace yourself**. Don't throw your life savings into a new token just because you read about it on social media. Experiment with small transactions, ask questions in communities, and learn from others' experiences.

Remember: Web3 is an adventure—part

technology, part social experiment, part financial frontier. By following this checklist, you'll build a foundation of knowledge and confidence, enabling you to fully experience the benefits of decentralized networks, communities, and marketplaces.

Final Reflections

Navigating Web3 for the first time can be like visiting a new country where the language, currency, and social norms all differ from what you're used to. But with the right preparation—securing your wallet, learning the basics of dApps and DAOs, and following a beginner's checklist—you can quickly become comfortable in this environment. Along the way, you'll likely discover fresh perspectives on ownership, community, and the role of technology in our lives.

Key Takeaways:

1. **Your Wallet Is Your Passport**: Choose

wisely, secure it, and keep your seed phrase private.

2. **dApps Unlock Decentralized Services**: From finance to art to social networks, the possibilities are vast, but proceed with caution.

3. **DAOs Offer Collective Ownership and Governance**: Joining one can be a rewarding way to meet like-minded people and shape real projects.

4. **Start Small, Learn Gradually**: Use the beginner's checklist to avoid getting overwhelmed or scammed.

5. **Stay Curious and Informed**: Web3 is constantly evolving, so be ready to adapt.

This chapter aims to give you tangible steps and a sense of security when venturing into Web3. The next question is: **where do you want to go?** Will you explore NFT art, dive deep into DeFi, join a global DAO tackling climate change, or simply dabble in a social dApp for the fun of it? The beauty of Web3 is that, for the first time, **the choice—and the control—truly rests in your hands**.

Chapter 8: The Future of Web3

Looking back on how the internet has evolved—from static web pages in the 1990s to the global social networks of the 2010s—it's evident that **change** is the only constant. Web3 represents the latest leap: a decentralized, user-owned internet that challenges the status quo of centralized platforms and data monopolies. But where do we go from here?

In this chapter, we'll dive into some of the **cutting-edge technologies** that could reshape Web3, examine the **challenges** that might slow its mainstream adoption, and envision the **potential impacts** on society, economics, and culture. While much of Web3 is still in flux, its continued development offers opportunities—and dilemmas—that no one can afford to ignore. Whether you're an enthusiast, a skeptic, or a curious observer, understanding these dynamics is crucial to staying informed about the next stage in the internet's evolution.

8.1 Emerging Technologies (Zero-Knowledge Proofs, AI Integration, etc.)

Web3 isn't static. As developers, researchers, and entrepreneurs continue to experiment, novel technologies arise that promise to **expand** its capabilities beyond the current scope of cryptocurrency trading, NFT marketplaces, and token-based communities. In this section, we'll explore **Zero-Knowledge Proofs, AI integration**, and several other developments that could redefine the Web3 landscape in the coming years.

8.1.1 Zero-Knowledge Proofs (ZKPs)

Zero-Knowledge Proofs (ZKPs) are a category of cryptographic techniques that allow someone to prove they possess certain information without revealing the information itself. Sounds paradoxical, right? But that's precisely what makes ZKPs so powerful.

1. **How They Work (High-Level)** Imagine a scenario where you want to prove you're over 18 without disclosing your exact birth date. With traditional methods, you hand over a driver's license or government ID, which includes not just your birth date but also your full name, address, and maybe even a photo. A ZKP-based system can confirm you're over 18 without exposing all those extra details. In more technical terms, you provide an encrypted "proof" that can be cryptographically verified, but no one sees the raw data.

2. **Why They Matter for Web3**

   o **Privacy Preservation**: One of the main criticisms of public blockchains (like Ethereum or Bitcoin) is that all transactions are out in the open. ZKPs can allow for private transactions or identity checks without sacrificing the security of the underlying blockchain.

o **Scalability**: Some ZKP solutions (like zk-rollups) can bundle multiple transactions off-chain, then post a succinct proof to the blockchain, significantly **reducing congestion** and **cutting fees**.

o **Regulatory Compliance**: In certain regulated scenarios, you need to prove compliance (e.g., verifying you're not a sanctioned individual) without revealing your entire financial history. ZKPs offer a path to bridging the gap between privacy and compliance.

3. **Real-World Examples**

- **Zcash**: A cryptocurrency focused on private transactions, employing ZKPs to hide transaction amounts and addresses.

- **zkSync**, **StarkNet**, **Polygon zkEVM**: Layer-2 solutions using ZKPs to improve Ethereum's throughput and lower gas costs.

Moving forward, ZKPs may underpin everything from **anonymous voting** in DAOs to **confidential** supply chain tracking, enabling a level of privacy previously unattainable on public blockchains.

8.1.2 AI Integration with Web3

Talk of **Artificial Intelligence (AI)** often conjures images of self-driving cars, advanced robotics, or generative text/image models. But how does AI intersect with Web3? Here are some compelling angles:

1. **Decentralized AI Platforms**

    o **Concept**: Imagine a network where data scientists and developers share algorithms and datasets without relying on giant corporations like Google or Amazon.

    o **Why It Matters**: AI research often requires vast datasets, which currently reside with tech giants. In a decentralized model, smaller players could pool resources to train more equitable AI models, governed by a tokenized incentive structure.

2. **Data Sharing and Monetization**

    o **Concept**: Users who **own** their data (see Chapter 6) might lease or sell it to AI developers under strict conditions. For instance, you could share your health data anonymously with a medical AI research program—earning tokens and advancing science, yet retaining control over how that data is used.

- o **Potential Impact**: This approach could decentralize the data monopoly, enabling more diverse AI training sets and possibly reducing bias in AI models.

3. **AI-Driven DAOs**

- o **Concept**: Future DAOs might incorporate AI "agents" that help analyze proposals, forecast outcomes, or detect fraudulent activity in real time. AI could also auto-generate suggestions or dynamic governance structures based on community sentiment.

- o **Concerns**: The "black box" problem

arises if humans rely too heavily on AI-based recommendations they don't fully understand. Ensuring transparency and accountability is key.

As AI algorithms become more sophisticated and require robust data sets, Web3's decentralized ethos and user-owned data solutions might pave the way for **collaborative AI** that benefits broader swaths of society, rather than consolidating power in the hands of a few major corporations.

8.1.3 Layer-2 Solutions and Multi-Chain Bridges

While not as headline-grabbing as AI or ZKPs, **Layer-2 (L2) solutions** and **multi-chain interoperability** are crucial for scaling Web3:

1. **Layer-2 Solutions**

    ○ **Role**: They process transactions off

the main blockchain (Layer-1) to reduce congestion and fees.

- o **Examples**: **Optimistic Rollups** (like Arbitrum, Optimism), **zk-Rollups** (like zkSync), and sidechains (like Polygon).

- o **Impact**: If mainstream adoption grows, blockchains need to handle millions of daily transactions. L2 solutions help scale without sacrificing security.

2. **Multi-Chain Bridges**

- o **Purpose**: Allow tokens and assets to move seamlessly between different blockchains (e.g., sending ERC-20 tokens from Ethereum to a Binance Smart Chain address).

- o **Challenges**: Bridges can be security hotspots. Several high-profile hacks have highlighted vulnerabilities. Despite these setbacks, robust bridging tech is vital for a future where multiple blockchains coexist, each specializing in different use cases.

As these technologies mature, end-users might not even realize they're using a complex web of blockchains. They'll just know dApps are faster, cheaper, and more interconnected—a leap forward in user experience.

8.1.4 Other Emerging Trends

- **Decentralized Identity (DID) Upgrades**
  Building on the concepts discussed in Chapter 4, DID solutions might integrate zero-knowledge credentials and AI-based verification. Expect improved user control and streamlined ways of proving credentials

across multiple platforms.

- **Quantum-Resistant   Cryptography**
  Quantum computing, if it becomes
  practically viable, could break classical
  encryption used by current blockchains.
  Researchers are developing quantum-
  resistant algorithms to future-proof
  blockchains.

- **Tokenized Real-World Assets (RWAs)**
  From real estate to precious metals, more
  real-world assets might be represented as
  tokens on a blockchain, simplifying
  fractional ownership, making it easier to
  trade or collateralize them in DeFi.

All these technologies share one common thread:
they push Web3 to be **more private**, **more
scalable**, **more accessible**, and **more aligned**
with real-world needs. However, grand
technological visions can only go so far without
addressing the very real obstacles to widespread

acceptance.

8.2 Challenges to Mainstream Adoption

Despite the excitement around Web3, **mass adoption** remains an uphill battle. In this section, we'll highlight the primary **challenges** that could slow Web3's integration into everyday life—ranging from user experience issues to legal and economic barriers.

8.2.1 Usability and Accessibility

Problem: Setting up wallets, managing seed phrases, and navigating dApps can feel like rocket science to newcomers. The average internet user is used to easy logins, password resets, and a friendly user interface.

1. **Complexity of Wallets**

   o Many first-time users accidentally

lose their seed phrases or fall victim to phishing sites.

- A portion of the population isn't comfortable with the idea of "being your own bank," and they'd prefer a customer support line.

2. **High Transaction Fees**

- During peak network congestion (especially on Ethereum), transaction fees can jump to tens or even hundreds of dollars, deterring everyday users who just want to send small amounts or play a casual blockchain game.

3. **Slow Speeds**

- Traditional credit card networks can handle thousands of transactions per second. Most blockchains currently handle far fewer, though Layer-2 solutions aim to fix this.

Potential Solutions: Layer-2 scaling, user-friendly wallet apps, social recovery mechanisms, and better user onboarding experiences. Projects like **Argent** (a mobile wallet) and **Rainbow** have made strides in simplifying the interface, but there's still a long way to go before your grandmother or neighbor can use Web3 without guidance.

8.2.2 Regulatory and Legal Uncertainty

Problem: Government agencies worldwide are still figuring out how to classify and regulate cryptocurrencies, NFTs, and DAOs. This uncertainty spooks potential investors, businesses, and mainstream users.

1. **Securities Laws**

   o Some tokens may be deemed securities (like stocks) if they're marketed as investments. This triggers strict compliance requirements that many Web3 projects aren't prepared to handle.

- Laws vary by country, creating a confusing patchwork of regulations for global users.

2. **Taxation**

- The question of how to tax crypto earnings—especially from yield farming, staking, or NFT flips— remains murky. Some jurisdictions treat every token swap as a taxable event, which can lead to complicated record-keeping.

3. **KYC/AML Requirements**

- Financial authorities want to prevent money laundering and terrorism financing. This may require dApps, exchanges, and DeFi platforms to collect personal identification information, potentially clashing with Web3's pseudonymous ethos.

4. **DAO Legal Status**

   o   DAOs operating across borders face issues of liability, corporate personhood, and contractual enforceability. Some are experimenting with legal wrappers (like the Wyoming DAO LLC in the U.S.), but there's no universal framework yet.

Potential Solutions: Collaborative efforts between regulators and Web3 leaders, clearer guidelines on token classifications, and the development of identity solutions that balance user privacy with compliance. Regulatory sandboxes— where governments let Web3 projects experiment under supervision—may also help create best practices without stifling innovation.

8.2.3 Security Concerns

Problem: Web3 is still a frontier. Hacks, scams, and rug pulls abound, and there's no centralized authority to reverse fraudulent transactions.

1. **Smart Contract Vulnerabilities**

   o Even well-known DeFi protocols have fallen victim to exploits in their code.

   o Small coding errors can lead to multi-million-dollar hacks.

2. **Phishing and Social Engineering**

   o Fake websites masquerade as real dApps to steal users' wallet credentials.

   o Scammers impersonate project administrators on Discord or

Telegram, tricking newcomers into handing over private keys.

3. **Bridge Attacks**

   o As mentioned earlier, cross-chain bridges can be a weak link. Hackers exploit vulnerabilities to siphon large sums of cryptocurrency.

4. **User Error**

   o In a system that emphasizes self-custody, losing your private key seed phrase can mean losing access to your assets forever.

Potential Solutions: More rigorous auditing of smart contracts, insurance protocols that reimburse users in case of a hack, advanced multi-signature wallet solutions, user education programs, and better user interface design that clarifies risky transactions.

8.2.4 Scalability and Environmental Concerns

Problem: The earliest blockchains, like Bitcoin and Ethereum (pre-Merge, for Ethereum), used Proof of Work (PoW) consensus mechanisms that require enormous energy consumption. While Ethereum's shift to Proof of Stake (PoS) has significantly reduced its carbon footprint, overall blockchain scalability and environmental impact remain topics of concern.

1. **Energy Use**

    o PoW blockchains use computational puzzles that consume huge amounts of electricity. Critics argue this is unsustainable, especially in a world that needs to cut carbon emissions.

    o PoS and other consensus models reduce energy usage, but not all chains have migrated yet.

2. Network Throughput

- With mainstream adoption, blockchains must handle **thousands** of transactions per second. Currently, many can't scale to that level without Layer-2 solutions or sidechains.

3. Public Perception

- High-profile negative press around energy usage or news of big hacks can taint the entire Web3 sector, discouraging eco-conscious or risk-averse users.

Potential Solutions: Migrating to more energy-efficient consensus models, adopting Layer-2 rollups, exploring alternative protocols like Directed Acyclic Graphs (DAGs), and implementing carbon offsets or using renewable energy sources. Overcoming these challenges will be key to building public trust and attracting businesses that prioritize sustainability.

8.2.5 Cultural and Educational Gaps

Problem: Many everyday users don't see the need for Web3. If they can pay for groceries, chat with friends, or watch streaming services easily through Web2, what's the incentive to switch?

1. **Lack of Awareness**

   o Web3 jargon—"gas," "seed phrase," "staking," "ZKPs"—confuses non-tech individuals. They might dismiss it as a niche fad or complicated gamble.

   o Mainstream media tends to focus on dramatic stories (like NFT million-dollar sales or crypto crashes), overshadowing real innovations.

2. **Education and Skill Shortages**

   o Schools and universities are only beginning to incorporate blockchain or crypto topics into curricula.

- o Employers struggle to find talent with both technical blockchain knowledge and user-centric design skills.

3. **Perception of Scams**

- o The frequency of rug pulls and fraudulent ICOs in past years has left a bad taste in many mouths. Some equate all of Web3 with get-rich-quick schemes.

Potential Solutions: Enhanced public outreach, simplified user interfaces that hide blockchain complexities, professional training programs, and mainstream media coverage that highlights genuine use cases rather than sensational headlines. In time, practical demonstrations (like real-world asset tokenization or effective philanthropic DAOs) might shift the perception from hype to tangible value.

8.3 Potential Impact on Society and Economy

While the challenges above are **significant**, the visionary potential of Web3 is equally monumental. If Web3 technologies manage to address usability, regulation, security, and scalability, they could usher in new ways of organizing economies, governing communities, and empowering individuals across the globe. Here, we'll look at **eight** key areas where Web3 could make a lasting mark.

8.3.1 Financial Inclusion and Access

1. **The Unbanked and Underbanked**

    o **Current State**: Billions worldwide lack access to stable banking systems or are subject to high fees and corruption.

- **Web3 Opportunity**: Decentralized finance (DeFi) could offer micro-loans, savings accounts, and remittance services without a traditional bank. People only need internet access and a crypto wallet.

- **Example**: A rural entrepreneur in Kenya could use a smartphone wallet to receive a micro-loan from a global pool of lenders, bypassing local banks with prohibitive interest rates.

2. **Remittances**

- **Issue**: Migrant workers often pay steep fees to send money home.

- **Web3 Solution**: Cross-border token transfers with minimal intermediaries, drastically cutting costs and speeding up delivery. Stablecoins pegged to fiat currencies can reduce volatility.

3. **Wealth Creation**

   o **Token Economies**: By tokenizing new types of assets or enabling play-to-earn games, individuals in developing nations might find fresh revenue streams.

   o **Risks**: Over-speculation and scams can also exploit vulnerable populations, so financial education is crucial.

If implemented responsibly, Web3 could provide essential financial services to those historically locked out by geography, bureaucracy, or bank policies.

8.3.2 Redefining Ownership and Data Rights

1. **Personal Data Markets**

- Instead of letting tech giants profit from your online activity, you could choose to monetize your own data or keep it private entirely.

- **Potential Shift**: We might witness a wave of user-controlled data exchanges. Marketers pay you directly for data insights, and you can revoke access at will.

2. **Intellectual Property and Royalties**

- **NFTs** already let creators embed royalties in digital assets so they get a cut each time the asset is resold.

- This could expand to music, videos, and other forms of media, ensuring artists continually benefit from secondary markets.

3. **Licensing and Rights Management**

- Complex licensing deals—for

software, images, or scientific patents—could be managed by smart contracts, ensuring each stakeholder automatically receives their share of revenue or usage rights.

In the long run, a world where your data, digital creations, and intangible assets are truly **yours**—tradeable and protectable on global marketplaces—could upend established business models and shift how society values digital identity and labor.

8.3.3 Transparent Governance and Civic Participation

1. **Voting Systems**

   o Blockchains could power tamper-proof voting for local councils, corporate shareholder votes, or even national elections—assuming robust identity verification and a user-friendly interface.

- o **Benefit**: Reduced election fraud, improved trust in outcomes, near-instant results.

2. **Public Funding and Grants**

- o DAOs could distribute public funds with unparalleled transparency. Citizens track exactly how tax revenue is allocated and vote on specific projects.

- o **Example**: A city adopting a "CityCoin" can reward civic engagement—like reporting infrastructure issues or volunteering in community projects.

3. **Collaboration Without Borders**

- o Decentralized governance models let people across countries coordinate on issues like climate change, disaster relief, or open-source projects.

o The global, permissionless nature of blockchain fosters cross-border alliances unthinkable in a purely nation-state centric environment.

If governments and civic institutions embrace at least some Web3 principles—like open ledgers for budgets or token-based voting—the result could be more democratic, accountable systems.

8.3.4 Shifts in the Creator and Gig Economies

1. **Creator Empowerment**

   o **Problem**: Many content creators rely on centralized platforms (e.g., YouTube, Patreon) that take large cuts or impose their own rules.

   o **Web3 Approach**: Creators can mint

NFTs for their work, launch social tokens, or join a DAO that governs their fan community. They interact directly with supporters, controlling revenue distribution.

2. **Play-to-Earn and New Gig Platforms**

   o Gamers can **earn tokens** or NFTs by playing. Workers might join decentralized freelancing platforms, earning crypto and governance rights.

   o **Caution**: Some models rely on continuous growth and can collapse if user engagement drops. Clear utility and sustainable economics are crucial.

3. **Micropayments**

   o Nano-transactions with negligible fees open doors to micro-tipping, pay-per-article reading, or streamed payments for online tasks.

- o This could spur new forms of side hustles and digital micro-jobs.

A more direct relationship between creators, consumers, and collaborators has the potential to dismantle gatekeeper platforms, though it also demands that creators navigate new complexities (managing tokens, marketing to crypto-savvy audiences, etc.).

8.3.5 Global Supply Chains and Logistics

1. **Traceability and Proof of Origin**

   - o With **blockchain-based record-keeping**, each step of a product's journey can be logged and verified, from raw materials to the retail shelf.

   - o **Consumer Impact**: Buyers see if their coffee truly comes from ethically sourced farms or if their clothes are produced under fair labor conditions.

2. **Reduced Fraud and Counterfeits**

   o NFTs or specialized tokens for luxury goods (handbags, jewelry) can verify authenticity. Once scanned, you know the item's full chain of custody.

   o This approach can also combat the spread of counterfeit pharmaceuticals or electronics.

3. **Logistical Efficiency**

   o Automated smart contracts could trigger instant payments to suppliers once goods arrive. This reduces paperwork, bureaucracy, and late fees.

Though companies like Walmart and Maersk have piloted blockchain tracking, broader adoption may accelerate if supply chain disruptions (like those seen during global crises) push industries to invest in more resilient, transparent systems.

8.3.6 Healthcare and Medical Data

1. **Patient-Centric Records**

   o Instead of hospitals owning your health records, you hold them in an encrypted identity wallet. You grant doctors or labs temporary access, and you revoke it once the consultation is done.

   o **Privacy Benefits**: Reduces the risk of large-scale data breaches. Patients also see who accessed their records and when.

2. **Clinical Trials and Research**

   o Transparent, tamper-proof data on patient outcomes can streamline drug development. Researchers verify data authenticity without revealing personal details.

- Token Rewards: Patients might earn tokens for contributing data to medical studies, offsetting the inconvenience of constant check-ups.

3. **Global Health Collaboration**

- Cross-border data sharing: If you're traveling and fall ill, local doctors can securely access your medical history.

- Real-time outbreak tracking: Public health agencies can log case data on a decentralized ledger, preventing underreporting or manipulation.

Privacy regulations (like HIPAA in the U.S.) complicate adoption, but the potential to **empower patients**, **reduce fraud**, and **improve health outcomes** is a compelling incentive for healthcare providers and governments to explore Web3 solutions.

8.3.7 Education, Credentials, and Skill Portfolios

1. **Verifiable Credentials**

   o Students receive **digital diplomas** on a blockchain. Employers verify them instantly, cutting out expensive background checks.

   o Certificates for online courses, workshops, or skill-based achievements become part of a personal, user-owned record.

2. **Peer-to-Peer Learning Platforms**

   o Tokenized incentives encourage learners to complete modules or help others, with micro-rewards for teaching or tutoring.

- **Open Curricula**: Educators from around the world collaborate to create comprehensive, peer-reviewed courses, funded by a DAO-like structure.

3. **Global Talent Matching**

- Imagine a decentralized LinkedIn where your verified skills, work history, and DAOs you've contributed to exist in your self-sovereign identity profile. Employers see validated track records, not inflated resumes.

By removing gatekeeping institutions and forging direct lines of verification between students and employers, Web3-based education models can empower lifelong learning and more equitable access to opportunities.

8.3.8 Macroeconomic and Social Transformations

Finally, if Web3 continues to expand, we could see a **paradigm shift** in how societies structure economic activity:

1. **Tokenized Communities**

   o Neighborhoods or cities might issue local tokens that fund community projects, reward volunteers, or attract tourism.

   o Global online communities run entirely by DAOs could rival traditional corporations in revenue generation, forming new "digital nations" with their own governance and economies.

2. **Reduced Reliance on Traditional Financial Institutions**

   o Banks and intermediaries might lose

some control if DeFi becomes robust enough to handle mainstream consumer lending, mortgages, or insurance.

o Central banks could respond with **CBDCs** (Central Bank Digital Currencies), integrating some features of blockchain but maintaining government oversight.

3. **Equitable Wealth Distribution or New Inequalities?**

o Advocates argue that token ownership by early adopters fosters wide "stakeholder capitalism," as more users gain shares in the platforms they use.

o Skeptics worry that whales (large token holders) could replicate the same inequality seen in Web2. Ensuring fair token distribution and governance remains a challenge.

As with any technological revolution, the outcomes for society depend on how we balance innovation, regulation, and collective responsibility. **Web3** could foster a world that's more inclusive, transparent, and community-driven—or it could simply replicate existing power imbalances in a shinier, more complex form.

Conclusion

The internet has come a long way since the days of dial-up modems and simple, text-based web pages. We've lived through the read-only Web1, witnessed the rise of user-generated content in Web2, and now find ourselves on the cusp of **Web3**—an internet defined by ownership, decentralization, and new forms of online collaboration.

Across these pages, we've seen how **blockchain**, **tokens**, **smart contracts**, and **user-owned data** form the bedrock of Web3's promise. We've explored how people can reclaim control over their digital identities, how communities can govern themselves through DAOs, and how entire economies might shift as tokens unlock new ways to incentivize participation and share value. Underneath the technical details and industry jargon lies a simple but powerful idea: the next generation of the internet is being shaped by **you**—

the user—rather than a handful of massive technology companies.

Why It Matters

Even if you don't consider yourself "tech-savvy," Web3 matters because it reimagines the power dynamics of our digital world. Rather than passively consuming content on someone else's platform, you can own a slice of that platform—or even create your own. Rather than surrendering your personal information to large corporations, you can store it yourself and choose how and when to share it. And rather than relying on gatekeepers to vet your identity or creativity, you can tap into global networks, where trust is enforced by transparent code and community consensus.

These shifts are, of course, **works in progress**. Web3 still faces hurdles: user-friendliness, security, regulatory clarity, and public perception. Not everyone sees the point of redesigning familiar online experiences, and others worry about scams or the financial speculation that sometimes overshadows genuine innovation. But as we've seen throughout this book, there's more to Web3 than pricey NFTs or convoluted token offerings. Beneath the hype lies a movement that strives to redistribute power and give individuals real choices about how they interact, contribute, and benefit in the digital realm.

Practical Takeaways

- **User Empowerment**: Owning your data, controlling your digital identity, and participating in token-based communities changes the online experience from "consumer" to "co-creator."

- **Tools and Tips**: From setting up a wallet securely to exploring dApps and marketplaces, you can start small and learn as you go. A few test transactions or an inexpensive NFT mint can teach you much more than reading a thousand articles.

- **Community Building**: Whether you join a DAO, launch your own token, or support a favorite artist's social token, Web3 brings people together around shared goals and ownership. It's less about hype and more about collective engagement.

- **Future Outlook**: Emerging tech like Zero-Knowledge Proofs, AI-driven dApps, and scalable Layer-2 networks will help address current limitations in privacy, speed, and cost. As these tools mature, expect Web3 to feel more intuitive and seamlessly integrated into everyday life.

Charting Your Own Path

Perhaps you're reading this book because you're curious how Web3 can help you start a business, support an artist you love, or protect your personal data. Maybe you're a skeptic, wanting to separate fact from fiction. Whatever your motivation, the best way to discover Web3's real potential is by

experiencing it. Set up a wallet, try a decentralized application, or dip your toes into a tokenized community. You don't need to invest large sums or become a coding wizard. Small, hands-on experiments can unlock understanding and spark your own creative ideas for how this technology might solve problems in your life, business, or community.

No one can predict exactly how Web3 will evolve in the coming years. We might see widespread adoption and a digital renaissance where individual creators and communities thrive as never before. Or we might see a more modest outcome, where only the most robust and user-friendly projects survive. But regardless of the ultimate shape Web3 takes, it has already reignited a sense of possibility and **reinvented the conversation** about who holds power in our digital spaces.

Final Thoughts

We stand at a crossroads where the internet's future

is not just an abstract concept but something each of us can influence. Web3 envisions a world where communities can collectively own platforms, governance is transparent, and individuals—not corporations—decide how personal data is shared. It challenges us to rethink long-standing norms around digital privacy, trust, identity, and value exchange.

It's an ambitious vision, and like any ambitious effort, it invites both excitement and skepticism. Yet, if one lesson stands out from the history of the internet, it's that **widespread change is possible** when technology aligns with human creativity and the desire for meaningful connection. Web3 might not be perfect, and it won't solve all our online woes overnight, but it presents a rare opportunity to reorient the web around the very people who use it.

So as you close this book, remember that **Web3 is still a conversation**—a global experiment unfolding in real time. There's a place for you in that conversation, whether you're an artist, a small business owner, a tech hobbyist, or just someone who wants more control and transparency in your online life. If any of the ideas here resonate, don't hesitate to jump in, learn more, and shape the future of the internet in a way that reflects your values and aspirations.

Ultimately, **the promise of Web3** isn't just about cryptography or blockchains. It's about reclaiming agency in a digital age—ensuring that our online world remains open, fair, and brimming with potential for all who seek to be part of it.

Glossary of Key Terms

Address

A unique string of characters—often a combination of letters and numbers—that represents where cryptocurrencies, tokens, or digital assets can be sent on a blockchain network. Think of it like a public-facing bank account number.

Airdrop

A method of distributing tokens (often for free) to a group of users or wallet addresses, usually as a promotional campaign or reward for early adopters. Users who receive an airdrop may gain voting rights or other benefits if they hold the token.

Blockchain

A decentralized digital ledger that records transactions in a series of "blocks." Once a block is finalized, it's chained to the previous one, making it extremely difficult to alter or tamper with past records. Bitcoin and Ethereum are examples of public blockchains.

Cold Wallet (Hardware Wallet)

A physical device (like a USB stick) that stores a user's private keys offline, providing added security. Since it's disconnected from the internet, it's much harder for hackers to access. Examples include Ledger and Trezor.

dApp (Decentralized Application)

A software application that runs on a blockchain or peer-to-peer network rather than a single, centralized server. Users typically interact with dApps by connecting their crypto wallets, allowing them to execute transactions or use the app's features without traditional logins.

DAO (Decentralized Autonomous Organization)

An online community or collective governed by

smart contracts and tokens rather than a traditional hierarchy. Members usually hold tokens that allow them to vote on proposals, allocate shared funds, and shape the DAO's direction collaboratively.

Data Ownership (User-Owned Data)

A principle in Web3 where individuals store and control their personal data, deciding who can access or use it. This stands in contrast to Web2, where large tech companies typically keep and monetize user data on their own servers.

DeFi (Decentralized Finance)

A broad category of dApps and protocols aimed at providing financial services—like lending, borrowing, or trading—without traditional banks or intermediaries. DeFi platforms use smart contracts to automate transactions, often rewarding users who provide liquidity or lock up (stake) their tokens.

DID (Decentralized Identifier)

A globally unique identifier (like did:example:12345...) that points to information controlled by the user rather than a central authority. Often used in self-sovereign identity systems, where you own the credentials that prove who you are, rather than relying on big tech logins.

Fungible Token

A type of token where each unit is interchangeable with another. Cryptocurrencies like Bitcoin (BTC) or Ether (ETH) are fungible—one BTC is the same as another. In contrast, see **Non-Fungible Token (NFT).**

Gas (Gas Fee)

A transaction fee paid on certain blockchains (like Ethereum) to compensate miners or validators who process and secure the network. Gas costs can fluctuate depending on network congestion. On Proof of Stake systems, these fees still apply but are often lower than older Proof of Work models.

Hardware Wallet

See **Cold Wallet**.

Hot Wallet (Software Wallet)

A crypto wallet that remains connected to the internet on a device such as a computer or smartphone. While more convenient for frequent transactions, it can be more vulnerable to hacking attempts compared to a cold (hardware) wallet.

InterPlanetary File System (IPFS)

A decentralized, peer-to-peer protocol for storing and sharing data, where each file is identified by a unique cryptographic hash. Instead of relying on a single server, IPFS breaks files into smaller chunks distributed across many nodes, aiming for censorship resistance and greater reliability.

Layer-1

A base blockchain or protocol (like Bitcoin or Ethereum) that processes and finalizes transactions on its own ledger. Layer-1 networks often face scalability challenges during high usage.

Layer-2

A secondary network or technology (like Optimistic Rollups, zk-Rollups, or sidechains) built on top of a Layer-1 blockchain to improve speed and reduce fees. Users typically perform most activities on Layer-2 while settling final transaction records on the main chain.

NFT (Non-Fungible Token)

A unique digital asset stored on a blockchain. Unlike fungible tokens, each NFT has distinct metadata that sets it apart—useful for items like digital art, collectibles, music, or in-game items that need to be one-of-a-kind or limited-edition.

Node

Any computer or server that participates in a blockchain network. Full nodes store the entire blockchain history and help validate transactions, while light nodes store only a portion of data for convenience.

Oracle

A service or mechanism that brings external, real-world data into a blockchain environment. Since smart contracts can't access the outside internet directly, oracles feed them necessary information (e.g., prices of assets, weather data, sports scores) to execute logic accurately.

Private Key

A secret code (akin to a very strong password) that grants you ownership and control of the digital assets linked to a corresponding public key or address. Anyone with your private key can move your tokens or NFTs, so it must be kept confidential and secure.

Proof of Stake (PoS)

A consensus mechanism where validators stake (lock up) tokens to secure the network and validate transactions. In return, they may earn rewards. This approach is more energy-efficient than Proof of Work and has been adopted by blockchains like Ethereum (post-Merge), Cardano, and Solana.

Proof of Work (PoW)

A consensus mechanism used by Bitcoin (and previously by Ethereum) that requires miners to solve complex mathematical problems to validate new blocks. It's secure but energy-intensive, leading many newer blockchains to adopt other methods (like PoS).

Rug Pull

A type of scam where a project's creators suddenly abandon it and run off with investors' funds, often after hyping a new token or NFT collection. Users are left with worthless assets and no recourse, emphasizing the need for due diligence and caution.

Seed Phrase (Recovery Phrase)

A series of 12–24 random words generated by your wallet that acts as a backup. If you lose your device, you can regenerate your wallet (including all tokens and NFTs) by re-entering this phrase. It's crucial to store it offline and never share it.

Smart Contract

Self-executing code deployed on a blockchain that automatically enforces rules and conditions. Think of it like a digital "if-then" agreement: when certain conditions are met, the contract triggers predefined actions (like sending funds, issuing tokens, or updating records) without human intervention.

Social Tokens

Tokens issued by an individual (like a musician, influencer, or community leader) or a group, meant to build loyalty, reward fans, or grant special perks. They often represent a personal or community brand rather than a purely financial investment.

Stablecoin

A type of cryptocurrency pegged to another asset—often a fiat currency like the U.S. dollar—to maintain a stable value. Examples include USDT (Tether), USDC (USD Coin), and DAI. They're commonly used to hedge against market volatility or conduct day-to-day transactions.

Token

A digital unit of value recorded on a blockchain. Tokens can be fungible (like ERC-20 tokens on Ethereum) or non-fungible (ERC-721 or ERC-1155 NFTs). They may represent cryptocurrencies, membership rights, governance power, or unique collectibles.

Tokenization

The process of converting assets or rights into a digital token on a blockchain. Tokenized real-world assets (like real estate or artwork) can be traded more easily, allowing fractional ownership and global liquidity.

Transaction

An instruction broadcast to the network, typically transferring tokens, minting NFTs, or calling a function in a smart contract. Each transaction must be validated by the blockchain's consensus mechanism and recorded in a block.

Wallet

An app or device for storing and managing private keys and digital assets. It lets you sign transactions, interact with dApps, and view your token balances or NFT collection. Wallets can be **hot** (software-based) or **cold** (hardware-based).

Web1

The early, "read-only" phase of the internet (1990s), dominated by static web pages and limited user interaction. Users primarily consumed content without the ability to interact or publish easily.

Web2

The "read/write" internet (2000s onward), where social media and user-generated content took center stage. Platforms like Facebook and YouTube let users post content and interact, but large tech companies typically controlled data and revenue streams.

Web3

The emerging, "read/write/own" internet characterized by decentralization, user-owned data, token-based communities, and smart contracts. Instead of centralized corporations controlling online platforms, networks are governed collectively, and users hold cryptographic keys to their digital assets.

Zero-Knowledge Proof (ZKP)

A cryptographic method that lets someone prove they know certain information (like a secret key or age qualification) without revealing the information itself. ZKPs are vital for enhancing privacy on public blockchains by enabling selective disclosure.

How to Use This Glossary

Refer back to these definitions whenever you come across unfamiliar words or acronyms. As Web3 continues to evolve, new terms and concepts will emerge, but many of these foundational ideas—blockchains, smart contracts, user-owned data—will remain central to understanding the next era of the internet.